James W. Moore

FAITH
Is the Answer,
but What
Are the
QUESTIONS?

D0062835

DIMENSIONS
FOR LIVING

NASHVILLE

FAITH IS THE ANSWER, BUT WHAT ARE THE QUESTIONS?

Library of Congress Cataloging-in-Publication Data

Moore, James W. (James Wendell), 1938-
    Faith is the answer, but what are the questions? / James W. Moore.
        p. cm.
    ISBN 978-0-687-64673-9 (binding: pbk., adhesive perfect : alk. paper)
    1. Christianity—Essence, genius, nature—Miscellanea. 2. Theology—Miscellanea. I. Title.
    BT60.M66 2007
    230—dc22

                                                                    2007009563

Portions of chapter 8: "Did Jesus Really Mean It When He Said, 'Love One Another'?" appear in *The Common People Heard Him Gladly: A Lenten Study for Adults* (Nashville: Abingdon Press, 2004).

09 10 11 12 13 14 15 16—10 9 8 7 6 5 4 3

MANUFACTURED IN THE UNITED STATES OF AMERICA

Contents

Introduction
Faith Is the Answer, but What Are the Questions?

Mark 10:17-22

As he was setting out on a journey, a man ran up and knelt before him, and asked him, "Good Teacher, what must I do to inherit eternal life?" Jesus said to him, "Why do you call me good? No one is good but God alone. You know the commandments: 'You shall not murder; You shall not commit adultery; You shall not steal; You shall not bear false witness; You shall not defraud; Honor your father and mother.' " He said to him, "Teacher, I have kept all these since my youth." Jesus, looking at him, loved him and said, "You lack one thing; go, sell what you own, and give the money to the poor, and you will have treasure in heaven; then come, follow me." When he heard this, he was shocked and went away grieving, for he had many possessions.

RECENTLY I RAN ACROSS A FASCINATING LIST OF UNUSUAL ANSWERS given by children on some tests at school. Let me share some of these with you.

In answer to the question "When was our nation founded?" one little boy wrote, "I didn't even know it was losted!"

In answer to a different question, another child said, "A *myth* is a female moth!"

Still another reported that Socrates died from an overdose of "wedlock"!

Asked to describe the famous painting of Whistler's mother, one student explained: "It shows a nice little lady sitting in a chair, waiting for the repairman to bring back her TV set!"

And then how about these interesting answers: "A horse divided against itself can't stand."

"The death of Thomas Jefferson was a big turning point in his life."

But here is my favorite. A little girl was asked to define the word *people*, and this is what she wrote:

"*People* are composed of girls and boys and men and women. Girls are nice. Boys are no good until they are grown up and married. My mother is a woman, which is a grown-up girl with children. My father is so nice that I think he must have been a girl when he was a boy!"

What we learn from this is that the right answers are important. But have you thought about this: So are the right questions! And one right question for us to ask is this: What does it really mean to be a Christian?

The well-known evangelist Billy Graham tells a wonderful old story on himself. It happened early in his ministry. He arrived in a small town to preach a revival. Early in the day, Dr. Graham was walking around on Main Street of the little town, looking for a place to mail a letter. He saw a little boy and asked him where the post office was.

The little boy said, "You go down Main Street for two blocks, turn right, go one block, then turn left, and you will see it right there on the corner."

Dr. Graham thanked him and said, "If you will come to the fairgrounds tonight at seven o'clock, you can hear me preach. I will be telling everyone how to get to heaven."

"I don't think I'll be there," the little boy replied. "*You* don't even know how to get to the *post office*!" The great thing about that story is that Billy Graham tells it on himself, with obvious fun and delight. But also, the story reminds us that all of us in this life are looking for something and that we need someone to help us find the way. We need someone to guide us and lead us and advise us and comfort us and encourage us. We need someone to save us from our lostness!

That was the rich young ruler's problem. He was lost. He couldn't find his way. He had all the things that our "Madison Avenue world" tells us we need in order to be happy—wealth, youth, and power—and yet despite having all of those things, he felt empty inside; he felt unfulfilled; he felt lost. Give him credit for this: He realized that the answer was with Jesus; he came to Jesus looking for help. But when Jesus told him, "Come and follow me, come and join me, come and walk with me and you'll have a richness of life that's just indescribable," the young man turned and walked away sadly.

Can't you see him? Shoulders slumped, eyes downcast, feet trudging away in sorrow, just bent over, the picture of defeat, emotionally spent, because he knew Jesus was right, but he just couldn't do it. He couldn't drop everything and put Christ first. He couldn't make that commitment, and he missed the new life that only Christ could give him.

In this young man's failure to respond and follow Jesus that day, we find some key insights into what it means to be a Christian, and they are all rooted in Jesus Christ. Let me show you what I mean with three thoughts.

First of All, Jesus Christ Is the One Who Shows Us the Way to Commit Our Lives to God

As portrayed in Irving Stone's *The Agony and the Ecstasy* (New York: Doubleday and Company, 1961), when Michelangelo was a young boy, he came to a master sculptor asking to be accepted as a student. The master sculptor told young Michelangelo that he did not know what he was asking or realize what sculpting means: "This will take your life!" Michelangelo replied, "What else is life for?"

This is what Jesus Christ teaches us about our commitment to God: What else is life for? Jesus shows us how to love God with all our heart, soul, mind, and strength, and to do it joyfully, saying, "What else is life for?"

Second, Jesus Christ Is the One Who Shows Us the Way to Love Other People

There's an old hymn that says it perfectly:

> Lord, help me live from day to day
> In such a self-forgetful way
> That even when I kneel to pray
> My prayer shall be for—Others.
> Others, Lord, yes, others
> Let this my motto be,
> Help me to live for others,
> That I may live like Thee.
> (Charles D. Meigs, "Others," 1917)

Look closely, now, at that last line: "That I may live like Thee." Jesus teaches us that the best way to show our love for God is to love others just as he did, tenderly, graciously, sacrificially, unconditionally.

Third and Finally, Jesus Christ Is the One Who Shows Us the Way to Celebrate Life

The joy of life is not in material things—they rust, they corrode, they break, and they go out of style. The real joy of life is found in following Jesus Christ. If you want meaning and purpose and fulfillment and zest and joy and power and excitement in your life, then follow Jesus. He is the way, the truth, and the life.

You want a great formula for life? Here it is: Life is worth living. People are worth loving. Jesus Christ is worth following. Follow him. Imitate him. Learn from him. Serve him. Trust him.

Some years ago, a fire broke out in a hotel in Chicago. Flames and smoke blocked the normal escape routes. Some people on the tenth floor went out onto a balcony to escape the smoke, but they were trapped there. It looked as if they were doomed.

However, one young man in the group braved the smoke and

went back into the building. Fortunately, he found an exit to a fire escape. Courageously, he made his way back through the smoke and flames and led the group to safety. Another person in the group later commented, "You can't imagine the feeling of relief and joy we felt when that young man came back for us and said, 'Follow me! I know the way!'"

This is what the Christian gospel says to us: Here is the One who knows the way to safety and life! Here is the One who can deliver you! Here is the One who can save you. Follow him and you can live. He will lead you to commitment, to love, and to life.

I believe that with all of my heart, but I also know that still we grapple with a number of tough questions daily in these challenging times. How does faith help us when problems arise? How does the Christian faith strengthen us when suffering or tragedy or heartache explodes into our lives? Did Jesus really mean for us to love everybody? How does the Holy Spirit help us? How do we keep our faith healthy? What in the world are we supposed to do as Christians? In this hectic world with so many things crying out for our allegiance and support, whom can we trust? These and other questions, we will deal with in this book.

Faith is the *answer*, of course, but still—what are the *questions*? And how do we respond to them honestly, creatively, and redemptively? That is the adventure before us in the pages that follow.

1

To Whom Will We Give Our Allegiance?

In Whom Will We Put Our Trust?

Deuteronomy 6:1-8

Now this is the commandment—the statutes and the ordinances—that the LORD your God charged me to teach you to observe in the land that you are about to cross into and occupy, so that you and your children and your children's children may fear the LORD your God all the days of your life, and keep all his decrees and his commandments that I am commanding you, so that your days may be long. Hear therefore, O Israel, and observe them diligently, so that it may go well with you, and so that you may multiply greatly in a land flowing with milk and honey, as the LORD, the God of your ancestors, has promised you.

Hear, O Israel: The LORD is our God, the LORD alone. You shall love the LORD your God with all your heart, and with all your soul, and with all your might. Keep these words that I am commanding you today in your heart. Recite them to your children and talk about them when you are at home and when you are away, when you lie down and when you rise. Bind them as a sign on your hand, fix them as an emblem on your forehead, and write them on the doorposts of your house and on your gates.

HER NAME WAS MARY LOU. HIS NAME WAS TOM. THEY WERE BOTH IN their eighties, and they were celebrating their sixtieth wedding anniversary.

A news reporter was there to cover the big event, and he asked this question: "Mr. Tom, so many marriages are failing today, and yet here you and your wife are, celebrating sixty years together. How did you do it? What is your secret?"

Mr. Tom didn't even have to think for a minute how to answer that question. Without a moment of hesitation, Mr. Tom said with a warm smile, "Well, the answer is on the face of my watch." He said, "Mary Lou's father gave me this watch as a wedding present on the day we were married, and over the years this watch has played a large part in giving us a happy marriage." The reporter didn't understand until he looked more closely. Inscribed across the face of the watch were these words: *Tom, tell Mary Lou you love her!*

Think of that—every time he looked to see what time it was over all of their sixty years together, there was that message from his father-in-law: *Tom, tell Mary Lou you love her!*

Tom's father-in-law was a smart man. He realized how much all of us need good reminders, how much all of us need to be constantly reminded of who we are and whose we are and what we should be about.

Two men were talking one day over lunch. The first man said, "My wife has a terrible memory, the worst memory I ever heard of." The second man asked, "Forgets everything, huh?" And the first man replied, "No—*remembers* everything!"

Most of us are the other way around. We are so forgetful. We just have a lot of trouble remembering things, and consequently we have to come up with all kinds of creative ways to remind us of what we need to be doing.

Some, of course, use the classic reminder of tying a string around their finger.

Others have gotten more technically advanced—they call themselves on the telephone and leave themselves a message in voice mail or on their home answering machine.

Others e-mail themselves a message reminder.

Some rely on their secretaries to remind them of their priorities of the day.

Others put a sticky note on the steering wheel of their car.

Still others write down a list and put it in their pocket—but then they have to tie a string around their finger or put a sticky note on the steering wheel to remind them to look at the list in their pocket!

Now, this problem of being forgetful is not a new challenge. It's as old as the Bible itself. That's precisely what this famous passage in Deuteronomy 6 is really all about. Moses is reminding the people that "the main thing is to keep the main thing the main thing"! He does this by giving them the Shema. It's recorded in Deuteronomy 6:4, one of the mountain-peak moments in all of the Bible, the Great Commandment of the Bible: "Hear, O Israel: The LORD is our God, the LORD alone. You shall love the LORD your God with all your heart, and with all your soul, and with all your might" (Deuteronomy 6:4-5).

Now, let me tell you why Moses is giving the people this Great Commandment at this time. Moses has led the people out of Egyptian slavery. They have been a nomadic people traveling in the wilderness for a long time, depending on God for everything, and now two very dramatic things are about to happen to them. First, they are about to cross over into the promised land. Second, Moses can't go with them. He has grown old and weak now, and Moses will not be with them to lead them into the promised land as they establish themselves there. Moses will not be with them to remind them constantly that they are God's covenant people, God's servant people, and they must put their trust in God and God alone.

So to help the people remember, Moses "ties a string around their finger" by giving them this Great Commandment to constantly remind them to put God first and to serve God alone and to put their faith and trust in God alone. "No other gods. Love God alone with all your heart, soul, and might." Put these words on the doorposts of your homes. Put these words on the gates of your city. Wear them on your armbands and headbands. Speak them in every worship service. Teach them to your children. Don't give in to the temptation to worship the gods of the Canaanites. Don't water down or contaminate your faith. Don't chase after every new fad that comes along. Just put your trust in Yahweh. Serve God and God alone.

For all those years, the Hebrew people had struggled to survive in the wilderness. Now, they have come to the promised land. They had dreamed of this. They had longed for this. They had prayed for this. But Moses knew that now, as they went into the land, they would face an even more dangerous problem: other people already lived there, and these people had their own set of gods they worshiped. They had a god of wine, a god of war, a god of fertility, and a god of this, that, and the other. And Moses knew that as his people settled in, some of these gods would look attractive to the Hebrews, so much so that they might begin to worship them. So Moses gave them this Great Commandment to be a constant and daily reminder to worship, serve, and trust God alone, to love God (and no other) with all your heart, soul, and might.

That Great Commandment is as relevant today as it was thousands of years ago when Moses first spoke it because it's all about choices, decisions, commitments, loyalties, and priorities. It's about deciding to whom will we give our allegiance; in whom will we put our trust? Let me bring this closer to home for us with three thoughts that emerge naturally out of this story of Moses and the Great Commandment.

First of All, When We Face an Uncertain Future, Remember God

As the Hebrew people marched into this new adventure in the promised land, with all of its challenges and uncertainties and new opportunities, Moses gave them the Great Commandment to remind them to put God first, to worship God alone, to not be taken in by false prophets or gimmicky religion, and to remember God's promise to always be with them.

Remember that scene in the great musical *The Sound of Music* where Captain von Trapp and Maria return from their honeymoon to discover that the Nazis have taken over Austria and that they are trying to force Captain von Trapp into their military service? The von Trapps have come to the abbey for refuge and to escape, but the nuns of the abbey tell them that all of the roadways are blocked at the border. Captain von Trapp decides that they will have to abandon their borrowed car and walk over the mountains the rest of the way. Maria is worried about the seven children making such a long, difficult and dangerous journey.

But then the kind Mother Abbess, quoting from Psalm 121:1, tells them, "You will not be alone. Remember, 'I will lift up mine eyes unto the hills from whence cometh my help.'... God be with you."

And off they go, into an unknown future, but confident that God will be with them and that God will see them through. And God did!

This is God's greatest promise, isn't it? We find it recorded over and over again in the Bible, on page after page of the Scriptures, God's promise to always be with us, God's promise to never forsake us, God's promise to give us the strength we need in every situation. Someone said that God always gives us the strength we need, but God doesn't give it to us in advance, or else we would take the credit.

So if you are going off to college or to a new school or a new job or a new marriage or a new home or a new location or a new challenge or a new opportunity or a new health situation, remember God. Remember God's love, strength, and great promise to always be with us.

That's number one: When you face an uncertain future, remember God, and trust.

Second, When We Are Tempted to Shortcut Our Best Selves, Remember God

When I was twelve years old, growing up in Memphis, Tennessee, I played one summer on a pretty good Junior League baseball team. That's what we called it back then, the Junior League; this was before Little League was created.

Our team representing the Hollywood section of Memphis made it all the way to the city championship game. In the last inning, we had a two-run lead with two outs, but the other team had the bases loaded. One more out was all we needed, and we would be city champs. The batter hit a routine ground ball to our third baseman. He fielded it cleanly and threw to first base. As our first baseman received the throw, the webbing in his glove broke, the ball went through, and before he could run and retrieve the ball, three runs had scored. The game was over, and we lost the city championship by one run!

In that game, I had been cleated by a runner sliding into second base. I stayed in the game, but I had a pretty deep cut on my leg. We were playing at the Memphis Fairgrounds, and the doctor who was on hand insisted that I go into the first-aid tent so that he could take a look at my leg. The coach told me to go on with the doctor. He said he would take my teammates on home (about a twenty-minute drive), and he would get somebody to wait for me and drive me home.

A few minutes later, as I came out of the tent, I couldn't believe my eyes. I couldn't believe who was waiting to drive me home in his truck. *How could the coach do this to me?* It was Mr. Tony. Mr. Tony was the last person I would have picked to drive me home. He was the town character, the town grouch! He was mean and tough, with a sour look and evil eyes. All of the young people and most of the adults in the Hollywood area of Memphis were scared to death of Mr. Tony. I was just twelve years old.

With fear and trembling, I got into the truck with Mr. Tony. With a frightened, squeaky voice, I said, "Thanks for waiting for me, Mr. Tony."

He grunted and scowled. For twenty minutes, we rode along in silence. It seemed like an eternity to me before we reached my house. As I got out of the car, I said, "Thanks for the ride, Mr. Tony." Mr. Tony looked at me with angry eyes, and he said, "So *that's* all you've got to say? 'Thanks'? How much gas do you think that's gonna buy?"

His harsh words were like a slap in the face, and I stammered, "I'm sorry, Mr. Tony. I don't have any money."

"Well, get on out of the truck!" he shouted.

I was hurt, stunned, and embarrassed. I got out of the truck and ran into the house. It was one of those awful, painful moments in life that you feel like you can never get over or forget. I dreaded seeing Mr. Tony after that, and I avoided him as much as I could, but when I did see him, the pain, the hurt, and the embarrassment would flood back into my mind.

Some years later, I was coming home from college for the weekend. When I arrived in Memphis, it was just getting dark. As I drove by the fairgrounds, I saw someone hitchhiking and holding up a sign that read *Hollywood*. I stopped, and—would you believe it?—the hitchhiker getting into my car, who do you think it was? That's right: It was Mr. Tony!

We rode along in silence. We came to my house and went on

down the road ten blocks or so further, and I pulled up right in front of Mr. Tony's house. As Mr. Tony started to get out of the car, he turned back and said, "Thanks a lot for the ride, Jim."

Now, you know what I wanted to say, don't you? Most every fiber of my being wanted me to say it. I was so tempted to say, "'Thanks'? 'Thanks'? How much gas do you think *that's* gonna buy?"

That's what I wanted to say. That's what I almost said, but just then I remembered something: I remembered God. I remembered Jesus and what he taught. I remembered my Christian faith, and, empowered by God's Holy Spirit, I said, "You are more than welcome, Mr. Tony! You can ride with me anytime! I'm always glad to help a friend!"

Moses knew the Hebrew people would face great temptations in their new land. He knew they would be tempted to do things not worthy of their sacred heritage. He knew they would be tempted to short-cut their best selves and contaminate their covenant faith. To fight that temptation off, Moses gave them this Great Commandment to love God alone with all their heart, soul, and might so that they would be sure to always remember God.

So, first, when we face the fears that go with the uncertainties of a new future, we can remember God with trust. And second, when we face the great temptations to be less than we are called to be, we can remember God with obedience.

Third and Finally, When We Have to Face Death, Then Too, Even Then, Especially Then, Remember God

Isn't it something to realize that Moses never made it to the promised land? He died just before they got there. He led the people out of Egyptian bondage. He led them through the Red Sea. He led them through the wilderness. He taught them how to be God's people. But when they came to a mountain where they could look over and see the new land, Moses realized that his body was old and weak and worn, and he didn't have the strength to go on. So he passed the torch to Joshua, and he let Joshua lead the people on into the land, while Moses stayed behind on the mountain alone to die.

Can you imagine how that must have felt for him, to be so near but yet so far, so close to the land he had dreamed of entering, and yet too old and too sick and too tired to go on? I can just imagine this conversation between Moses and God. I can hear Moses saying, "Lord, I know your plan is best, but I can't help but feel disappointed. I wanted so much to lead the people into the land. I had dreamed of that. I wanted that so badly, and now this. I'm so weak, so frail, so tired. If only I could have had a little more time."

And God answers, "Moses, Moses, you have served me well. You have done your best. It will very soon be time for you to come and live with me."

Moses looks down from the mountain, and he sees the people moving forward toward the promised land without him, and suddenly Moses feels so alone. Moses looks up to heaven, and quietly he says, "Are you with me, Lord? Are you with me?"

And the answer comes back: "Of course I am, Moses. Of course I am."

This is the good news of our faith. When we have to face an uncertain future, when we have to do battle with temptation, and, yes, even when we have to face our own death or the death of a loved one, we can remember God and the great promise to always be with us, and we can remember to love God with all our heart, soul, and might.

2

Why Believe in Jesus?

Acts 16:25-34

About midnight Paul and Silas were praying and singing hymns to God, and the prisoners were listening to them. Suddenly there was an earthquake, so violent that the foundations of the prison were shaken; and immediately all the doors were opened and everyone's chains were unfastened. When the jailer woke up and saw the prison doors wide open, he drew his sword and was about to kill himself, since he supposed that the prisoners had escaped. But Paul shouted in a loud voice, "Do not harm yourself, for we are all here." The jailer called for lights, and rushing in, he fell down trembling before Paul and Silas. Then he brought them outside and said, "Sirs, what must I do to be saved?" They answered, "Believe on the Lord Jesus, and you will be saved, you and your household." They spoke the word of the Lord to him and to all who were in his house. At the same hour of the night he took them and washed their wounds; then he and his entire family were baptized without delay. He brought them up into the house and set food before them; and he and his entire household rejoiced that he had become a believer in God.

SOME YEARS AGO ON A RANCH IN SOUTH TEXAS, AN ELDERLY WOMAN was critically ill. She was in her nineties and was at the point of death. All of the family, the ranch hands, and the neighbors had gathered around her bed. Quietly, respectfully, they waited and watched and prayed. The doctors had told them that the end was near, nothing else could be done medically, and it wouldn't be long now.

Suddenly, there was a knock at the front door. It was a traveling revival preacher. He had arrived in the nearby town that morning, and someone had told him about the woman and how seriously ill she was.

The traveling preacher had come right out to the ranch. He went to the woman's sickbed and took hold of her hand. Weakly, she opened her eyes and asked him, "Who are you? I don't know you."

The revival preacher patted her hand and in a very sanctimonious tone, he said to her, "They tell me you don't have much time left. You are approaching death fast now, and I have come to forgive your sins and to get you ready to meet your Maker."

The elderly ranchwoman suddenly sat up in bed, and firmly she said to the revival preacher, "Let me see your hands." She took a quick look at the preacher's hands, and then, resolutely, she said, "You, sir, are an imposter!"

"Pardon me?" answered the preacher.

"You, sir, are an imposter!" she said a second time, and then she added, "Only that One with nail prints in his hands can forgive my sins! Only that One with nail prints in his hands can get me ready to meet my Maker!"

Let me ask you something: Do you know up close and personal that One with nail prints in his hands? Have you felt personally the forgiveness that comes only from the One who has nail prints in his hands? Are you totally committed to him?

Jesus' early followers were! They literally gave their lives for the cause of Christ. Why? Because they were unflinchingly committed to Jesus, and they believed with all their heart that they were continuing his ministry of faith, hope, and love. They were absolutely convinced that Jesus would always be with them in this world and in the world to come and that ultimately he would give them the victory. So they had a poise, a serenity, a determination, a courage, and a confidence that enabled them to do their best and then trust God for the rest.

We see a powerful example of this "blessed assurance" in Acts 16. Remember the story with me.

Paul and Silas had gone to Philippi on a preaching mission. While there, a young girl, a slave, pestered Paul because he was preaching about Jesus. This girl's mind was disturbed, but she had the reputation of being a fortune-teller, and she was bringing in a lot of money for her owners, the Scripture tells us, as people would come to her and pay to have their fortunes told.

But then one day, Paul stopped his preaching long enough to heal the girl's troubled mind. When her owners saw that she was now in her right mind, they were afraid she wouldn't be able to tell the future anymore, and their hope of making money through her might be gone. So they turned on Paul and Silas in anger and brought charges against them.

Paul and Silas were arrested immediately. They were stripped and beaten severely with rods. Then they were thrown into prison. The jailer was ordered to keep them securely, so to be safe he put their feet in stocks and placed them in a tightly locked cell. But despite all that had happened, with surely more troubles to come, Paul and Silas displayed that amazing courage and confidence so characteristic of those early church leaders.

At midnight, they were praying and singing hymns to God and sharing their faith with the other prisoners. Suddenly, there was an earthquake—an earthquake so violent that the prison cell doors ripped open, and the chains and stocks holding Paul and Silas broke and fell off.

The jailer woke up from a deep sleep and saw that the cell doors had been opened. He thought Paul and Silas had escaped and believed that he would be in big trouble with the authorities because the prisoners had escaped on his watch. The jailer was so scared, so upset that he would be held responsible for their escape, that he drew his sword to take his own life. But Paul saw what he was about to do and shouted to him, "Wait! Wait! Don't harm yourself! It's okay! We are all still here!"

The jailer was astonished by their faith! Their amazing response, their courage, their self-assurance, their compassion toward him touched the jailer's heart. He ran into the cell where Paul and Silas were and said, "Sirs, what must I do to be saved?" They told him to believe in the Lord Jesus Christ, and that very night, the jailer and his whole family accepted Christ and were baptized.

The next morning, the authorities realized that Paul and Silas were Roman citizens. The police were embarrassed and scared because they had done this to Roman citizens, so they came, apologized, and released them.

Now, the question that erupts out of this story is this: Where did Paul and Silas get that power, that power that so touched and impressed the jailer? What was the secret of their strength? What gave them their courage, their confidence, and their compassion? You know the answer to that, don't you? They got it from their faith. They got it from their church. They got it from Jesus because Jesus gives to all of us who follow him three incredible gifts: a self you can live with, a faith you can live by, and a love you can live out. Let's take a look at each of these.

Gift Number One: A Self You Can Live With

Some time ago, I went to Grace Theater in Houston to see the A.D. Players' production of *Godspell*. This play has so many wonderful moments. One of my favorites is that scene toward the end when Jesus is with his disciples in the Upper Room. Jesus takes a bucket of water, a rag, and a mirror, and he goes to his disciples, each in turn, and washes away their clown faces. Then, he holds the mirror up in front of them, so they can see themselves as they really are, and then he hugs them!

The point is clear and obvious and powerful: We don't have to wear false faces, we don't have to hide our inadequacies, and we don't have to pretend to be something we are not. God loves us and accepts us just as we are! There's a name for that. It's called amazing grace. It's called acceptance. It's called forgiveness. It's called unconditional love. And when we realize that this is precisely the way God loves us through Christ, it sets us free. It frees us from the tyranny of the past. It gives us a self we can live with.

That's exactly what happened to Paul on the Damascus Road. Known as Saul at the time, he had been out there like a one-man vigilante, a self-appointed bounty hunter, trying to single-handedly stamp out this new little nuisance group who were calling themselves Christians. He had a harsh, violent mind-set, a "Let's mow 'em down before they get out of hand" mind-set. "All of this talk about

Jesus and resurrection has got to stop, and I'm just the man to do it," Paul said outwardly; but inwardly, Paul wasn't feeling too good about himself. The disciple Stephen had gotten to him! Paul had stood there and held men's coats as they stoned Stephen to death, and Stephen prayed for those who were killing him: "Father, forgive them. They don't understand. Father, don't hold this against them." Paul would never forget that scene. He couldn't get over that. No fear and trembling, no crying out, no curses or screams, just that gracious spirit saying, "Lord, forgive them." Paul couldn't get over that because he knew Stephen had something he didn't have. Paul was deeply troubled, deeply burdened by that.

And then came the Damascus Road experience, where Paul came face-to-face with the risen Lord, the one he had been persecuting, and was converted, changed, turned around (see Acts 7:54-60; 8:1-3; 9:1-19a). Frederick Buechner described it like this in his colorful way:

> Paul waited for the axe to fall. Only it wasn't an axe that fell. "Those boys in Damascus," Jesus said. "Don't fight them, join them, I want you on my side," and Paul never in his life forgot the sheer lunatic joy and astonishment of that moment.... He was never the same again, and neither, in a way, was the world.
>
> Everything he ever said or wrote or did from that day forward was an attempt to bowl over the human race as he'd been bowled over himself.... And grace was his key word.... And Christ was his other key word, of course.... He never forgot how [the risen Christ] called him by name—twice, to make sure it got through—and [later he wrote] ... "I have been crucified with Christ ... it is no longer I who live but Christ who lives in me."
> (Frederick Buechner, *Peculiar Treasures* [San Francisco: Harper & Row, 1979], 129-31)

Have you heard the old story about the drunken man who fell asleep in a hotel lobby? While in his drunken stupor, some teenage pranksters rubbed Limburger cheese on the man's upper lip. When he woke up, he smelled this terrible odor, and he said, "This hotel smells awful!"

Then he went outside and still smelled the odor, and he cried, "This neighborhood smells terrible!"

13

He walked a few blocks away. The stench was still there, and he said, "This city smells rotten!"

Then he ran outside the city limits trying to get away from this awful odor, but he found it was still there. In despair, the drunken man shouted, "This whole world stinks!"

But you see, it doesn't; the problem was on his own upper lip. So often this is true. The problem is not "out there." It's in here in our hearts. This was Paul's problem. He wasn't happy with himself, so he took it out on the Christians. But then the risen Christ came looking for him and said, "Paul, I know what you've been doing. I know you've been working against me, but I still love you and want you with me. I want you on my side."

That moment turned it all around for Paul. The whole world didn't stink anymore. Paul felt loved, accepted, wanted, needed, and forgiven, and he became a new person. Saul the persecutor became Paul the missionary. Saul, the man filled with hostility, became Paul, the man who wrote what is known as the Love Chapter of the Bible (1 Corinthians 13)! Why? Because Jesus, the risen Christ, had given him a self he could live with, and you know, Jesus can do that for you. He can give you a self you can live with.

Gift Number Two: A Faith You Can Live By

The jailer was impressed by the faith of Paul and Silas, inspired by the way Paul and Silas lived their faith even in a tough situation.

Our granddaughter, Sarah, loves to create. She constantly draws cartoons and greeting cards and signs and posters. One day when she was eleven years old, she made a poster that she entitled "Why Kids Get Spooked." In answer to that implied question, she wrote "Kids get spooked by watching scary movies at night; 98.5 percent of kids get spooked by scary movies, and then they see frightening illusions in the darkness. So, parents, be sure to check the ratings before taking your children to a movie." At the bottom of the poster, Sarah wrote: "Turn Page Over for Rating System." On the back of the poster, she wrote the following:

G—Take Your Kids

PG—Know Your Kids

PG-13—Don't Take Kids Under 13

R—Bad Idea

NC–17—Hire a Sitter!

Even though she was only eleven years old, Sarah realized that we all need guidelines for living. As Christians we are so fortunate in this respect because we have Jesus. Jesus died on the cross to save us, but he also came and lived among us to show us God's will, to show us how God wants us to live. Christianity is not just a creed we profess; it is a lifestyle we live, the lifestyle of continuing the ministry, the witness, the truth, and the influence of Jesus. That's what Paul and Silas were doing that night in their prison cell. They were emulating their Lord.

Everywhere we go these days, we see young people wearing necklaces and T-shirts with the letters *WWJD*. The letters stand for "What Would Jesus Do?" These young people are trying to remember to measure their actions, their decisions, their choices, and their attitudes by the truth of Jesus Christ. "What would Jesus do?"

Jesus is our guide, our teacher, our measuring stick. The measuring stick of Christ tells us to be committed to God, to be compassionate toward others, to be loving, caring, and kind, to be just and fair and honest and truthful, to be loyal and merciful and gracious. Anything that doesn't measure up to that is wrong and sinful! So we can put our trust and confidence in the promise of God to always be with us and in the truth of Christ to always guide us because Jesus gives us a self we can live with and a faith we can live by.

Gift Number Three: A Love You Can Live Out

The jailer was surprised by Paul's and Silas's love for him and compassion toward him, but we are not surprised because we know that they were followers of Jesus. That's what the followers of Jesus do.

They reach out in love and compassion to others. Authentic followers of Jesus serve as the conduits of his love, the instruments of his compassion.

Dr. Charles Allen, in his book *The Miracle of Love* (Old Tappen, N. J.: Fleming H. Revell Company, 1972), shares a story about a man visiting with a little girl. She was showing the man her doll collection. She had dolls of all shapes, sizes, and textures and was so proud of her dolls.

"Which one is your favorite?" The man asked.

"Promise you won't laugh if I show you?" replied the little girl.

"I promise," he said.

The little girl ran out of the room, and in a moment she returned with a doll that looked like it had come from the world's worst garage sale. It was bald, broken, and scratched. Its clothes were frayed, and two limbs were missing.

"Out of all your dolls," said the man, "tell me why you love this one the most."

The little girl said, "I love this one the most because I'm afraid that if I don't love her, no one else will!"

Now, let me ask you something. Where did that little girl learn to love like that? You know, don't you? She learned it at church, at Sunday school. She learned it from Jesus.

A lot of people in this world sometimes feel the way that doll looked—worn, tattered, and used. They are the ones who need our love most of all. They are the ones who need to feel the loving touch of the Master's hand through us. If we don't love them, who will?

This was the power Paul and Silas had, the power that gave them courage and confidence, the power that inspired a jailer, the power that comes from Jesus. Because, you see, he gives to all of his followers these three amazing gifts—a self you can live with, a faith you can live by, and a love you can live out.

3

What Does It Mean to Build Your Life on Jesus Christ?

John 15:1-5

"I am the true vine, and my Father is the vinegrower. He removes every branch in me that bears no fruit. Every branch that bears fruit he prunes to make it bear more fruit. You have already been cleansed by the word that I have spoken to you. Abide in me as I abide in you. Just as the branch cannot bear fruit by itself unless it abides in the vine, neither can you unless you abide in me. I am the vine, you are the branches. Those who abide in me and I in them bear much fruit, because apart from me you can do nothing."

ROSEMARY BROWN IS A HIGHLY RESPECTED MINISTER. SHE HAS BEEN featured a number of times on The Protestant Hour national radio broadcast. She tells a story about a little four-year-old girl in her church, a precious, adorable, outgoing little girl who loves to sing.

One Sunday morning, this young girl ran down to the front of the sanctuary just before the start of the morning worship service, and excitedly she said, "Miss Rosemary Brown, can I sing a song this morning?" Not wanting to say no to this vivacious little girl, Rosemary said, "Of course you can." Then, Rosemary announced to the congregation that the young girl would sing the Call to Worship to start the service.

Rosemary Brown picked up the little girl and stood her on the front pew. The four-year-old turned around to face the now smiling congregation that day and sang: "Jesus wuvs me, dis I know, for da Bible tells me so. Yes, Jesus wuvs me." And then, she threw her hands straight up in the air (as though she had just scored a touchdown), and with a triumphant voice, she said, "And dat's dat!" And then the girl sat down (Rosemary Brown, "The Apple of My Eye," *The Protestant Hour*, 3/14/2005, 3).

That little girl was right on target, wasn't she? What more do we need to know? Jesus loves us, and that's that. When we are scared or confused or lonely, when we have to make a hard decision or face a tough challenge, when we feel rejected or cast aside by someone, when we lose a loved one or face our own death, what more do we need to know? Jesus loves us, and that's that!

But the problem is that sometimes we forget that; sometimes we turn away from Christ and look for love and happiness and meaning and excitement and fulfillment in other places. We come up empty, we come up frustrated, and we come up disillusioned.

Have you heard the story about the man who ordered a tree house over the Internet? When the box arrived, it had printed on the top the words that have become every parent's nightmare: *Some Assembly Required.*

The man began to assemble the tree house, but—would you believe it?—as he laid out all the parts on the floor and began reading the instructions, he realized, to his dismay, that the instructions were indeed for a tree house, but the *parts* were for a *sailboat!*

The next day, the man sent an angry e-mail message to the company complaining about the mix-up. Back came the reply: "We are truly sorry for the error and the mix-up and the inconvenience. However, it might make you feel better to consider the fascinating possibility that somewhere today there is a man out on a lake trying to sail your tree house."

The point is clear: To put something together, you have to have the right parts and the right instructions. This is where faith comes in. The only way you can put your life together is through faith, faith in Jesus Christ, our Lord and Savior. That's what makes it work. That's the way to assemble your life. Root it in Jesus Christ; tie it to Jesus Christ; ground it in Jesus Christ.

WHAT DOES IT MEAN TO BUILD YOUR LIFE

Max Lucado, in his book *When God Whispers Your Name,* puts it dramatically and graphically like this:

> Take a fish and place him on a beach. Watch his gills gasp and scales dry. Is he happy? No! How do you make him happy? Do you cover him with a mountain of cash? Do you get him a beach chair and sunglasses? ... Do you wardrobe him in double-breasted fins and people-skinned shoes?
> Of course not! Then how do you make him happy? You put him back in his element. You put him back in the water. He will never be happy on the beach simply because he was not made for the beach. (Max Lucado, *When God Whispers Your Name* [Dallas: Word Publishers, 1994], 173)

Indeed so and the same is true for you and me. We will never be happy living apart from the One who made us and saved us. Just like a fish was made to live in water, we were made to live in close fellowship with our Lord, and nothing can take the place of that.

That's what this passage in John 15 is all about. Just a few days before the Crucifixion and the Resurrection, Jesus said to his disciples, "I am the vine, you are the branches." In other words, "Stay connected to me, and you will live and thrive and bear fruit. Apart from me, you will wither and die."

The apostle Paul spoke about that in his writings. Let me paraphrase him like this: "I gave you a good foundation—Jesus Christ. You build on Jesus Christ. If you build with gold and silver or straw, it will fade. You must build your life on Jesus Christ. Stay connected to him."

Staying connected to Christ is so crucial for us as Christians. Let me show you what I mean with three thoughts.

First of All, Stay Connected to Christ's Servant Mentality

Serving others, loving others, reaching out to others, helping others—this was without question the approach, the lifestyle, Jesus chose.

In his book *Living on Tiptoe* (Waco, Tex.: Word Books, 1972), Cecil Myers reminds us of a time when a group of educators at the

19

University of Chicago wanted to honor Albert Schweitzer, and they brought him to America to give him an honorary degree. When Albert Schweitzer's train arrived, the university leaders ran to greet him warmly, and they told him how pleased they were that he was here in America.

But then as they turned to leave the train station, suddenly Albert Schweitzer was gone. He just disappeared, vanished, slipped away. They looked everywhere for him. Finally, they found him. He was carrying a suitcase for an elderly woman. He had seen that she was having trouble and had rushed over to help her.

You see, it was so much a part of Albert Schweitzer's life to be a servant for others that when he got off the train, it was as natural as breathing for him to begin immediately to look for somebody to help. That was his approach to life, and he had learned that from the Bible; he had learned that in church. He had learned that from Jesus. Albert Schweitzer loved to help other people because he was strongly connected to Christ and to Christ's servant mentality. The university officials said later that when they saw Dr. Schweitzer helping that woman with her suitcase, they were wishing like everything that they could find somebody they could help, somebody whose suitcase they could carry.

Put that over against this. Some years ago, Mother Teresa was asked by a reporter, "What is your biggest problem?" Without a moment of hesitation, Mother Teresa answered with one word: "Professionalism." She said,

Here are these servants of Jesus who care for the poorest of the poor. I have one who just went off and came back with her medical degree. Others have come back with registered nurse degrees. Another with a master's in social work, and when they came back with their degrees, their first question always is, "Where is my office?" Then she said, "But you know what I do? I send them over to the House of the Dying where they simply hold the hands of dying people for six months and after that, they're ready to be servants again." (Victor D. Pentz, "Take This Job and Love It," *The Protestant Hour,* 3/14/2005, 3)

This was the greatness of Mother Teresa, her unflinching commitment to stay connected to Christ's servant mentality.

That's your calling and mine as Christians—not to be prima donnas, but to be Christlike servants, servants strongly and unwaveringly connected to Christ's servant mentality.

Some years ago, I was walking up to the building where our Texas Annual Conference was being held. A young woman was just behind me. I held the door open for her. She was offended by that, and she said, "You didn't have to hold the door open for me because I'm a woman." And I said, "I didn't hold the door open for you because you are a woman. I held the door open for you because you are a person. I learned in Sunday school long ago to be a courteous and polite servant to everybody. If you had been a man, I would have held the door open for you." And she said, "Cool!"

Well, it is "cool" when we stay connected to Christ's servant mentality, when we get up in the morning and go through the day looking constantly (as naturally as breathing) for ways we can be Christlike servants.

Second, Stay Connected to Christ's Great Promise

After the Resurrection, Christ reassured and encouraged the disciples and told them to take up his ministry, and then he gave them his great promise: "Remember, I am with you always" (Matthew 28:20). That promise, "Christ's presence always with them," is what kept the early disciples going. It gave them strength and assurance and hope and courage and comfort and inspiration. That's exactly what it does for us too, so we need to stay strongly and unwaveringly connected to Christ's great promise: "I will not leave you alone. I am with you always."

The apostle Paul later put it like this: "Nothing can separate us from the love of God in Christ Jesus, our Lord" (see Romans 8: 37-39).

Her name is Jan Lancaster. She lives in Michigan. There was an economic recession, and Jan's husband lost the job he had held for eighteen years. Without income, Jan and her husband soon lost their home.

Jan became angry with God. They didn't deserve this. Why did God allow this to happen to them? Jan became so depressed and disillusioned that it took its toll and had an impact on her relationship with God. Even in the depths of despair, Jan still had faith that somehow God would help her family turn their lives around, and that somehow God would help them find another home. But Jan was impatient. She wanted to see evidence of God's concern immediately. A few years later, Jan, her husband, and their nineteen-year-old daughter moved into a new home. As Jan was lining the kitchen shelves with paper, she became frustrated because she could not get the paper to stay flat. She started over, folding and pressing one small section at a time. This method worked very well, and suddenly, right there in her new kitchen, Jan was struck by a powerful insight.

> Suddenly, it was clear to me that this was very much how the Lord had brought us through the last three years—one small step at a time, teaching and leading us day by day.
>
> I started to cry as I thanked God for bringing us through. I saw the closeness [grow within my family] ... Most important, I could see that no matter what happens in my life, what is added on or taken away, God will be there with me. (Jan Lancaster, "Angry at God," *Upper Room*, March/April 1993, 9)

"Remember, I am with you always"; that is the great promise of Christ to us, and it is crucial that we as Christians stay strongly connected—first, to Christ's servant mentality, and second, to Christ's great promise to always be with us.

Third and Finally, Stay Connected to Christ's Amazing Grace

There's an old story about a minister who dreamed that he had died and that he was trying to get into heaven. When he approached the gates, Saint Peter told him he needed 100 points to get in.

Proudly, the minister said, "Well, I was a minister for forty-three years."

"That's fine," said Saint Peter. "That's worth one point."

"*One point?* Is that all?" cried the minister. "Just *one point* for forty-three years of service?"

"Yes, that's correct," answered Saint Peter.

"Well, I visited shut-ins."

"One point."

"I worked with young people."

"One point."

"I developed a number of fine Scout programs."

"One more point. That makes four points; you need ninety-six more."

"Oh, no!" said the minister, in a panic. "I feel so helpless, so inadequate. Except for the grace of God, I don't have a chance!"

And Peter replied, "'Grace of God,' ninety-six points; *come on in!*"

Now, that minister's dream has some bad theology and some good theology in it. The bad theology is that we *don't* work our way into heaven by earning points. We do good works not in order to gain heaven, but in gratitude for what God has already done for us in Christ. The good theology here is that our only hope is the grace of God, the amazing grace of God in Jesus Christ. Like the minister said, "Except for the grace of God, we don't have a chance."

But the good news is, we have God's grace. We have God's grace because "God so loved the world that he gave his only Son, that whoever believes in him should not perish" (John 3:16 RSV). So the point is clear. If we are to stay alive and well, if we are to thrive and produce good fruit in this world, if we are to remain spiritually healthy and whole, then here's the formula, in John 15: Stay connected to the true vine, stay connected to Christ's servant mentality, stay connected to Christ's great promise to always be with us, and stay connected to Christ's amazing grace, remembering always that Jesus loves us, and that's that!

4
When Do We Feel God's Pleasure?

Matthew 3:13-17
Then Jesus came from Galilee to John at the Jordan, to be baptized by him. John would have prevented him, saying, "I need to be baptized by you, and do you come to me?" But Jesus answered him, "Let it be so now; for it is proper for us in this way to fulfill all righteousness." Then he consented. And when Jesus had been baptized, just as he came up from the water, suddenly the heavens were opened to him and he saw the Spirit of God descending like a dove and alighting on him. And a voice from heaven said, "This is my Son, the Beloved, with whom I am well pleased."

JERRY SEINFELD ONCE SAID, "MEN DON'T WANT TO KNOW WHAT'S ON TV, they want to know *what else* is on TV!" That explains one night recently why I was channel surfing with my television remote control. Suddenly, there it was, the great movie *Chariots of Fire*. It was released in 1981 and went on to win four Academy Awards, including one for Best Picture. The film is based on a true story about the Olympic Games of 1924.

One of the main characters in the movie is a young man from Scotland named Eric Liddell. Eric is doing his college work in Edinburgh, preparing himself to be a Christian missionary in China. He is also preparing to represent Great Britain in the Olympics. He is a world-class sprinter who runs with joy and reckless abandon, and he does become an Olympic champion.

When my channel surfing produced *Chariots of Fire* (as luck would

25

have it), I just happened to hit it right at the beginning of one of my favorite scenes in the film. It's a classic scene, especially for us as Christians. Eric Liddell is standing on a beautiful Scottish hillside. He is visiting with his sister Jennie. Off in the distance, you can see the skyline of Edinburgh, Scotland. Eric and Jennie are talking about his future. Jennie reminds Eric about his call to be a missionary in China. She questions him about the time he is spending on all of this running, as he prepares for the Olympics. Eric responds with one of the greatest "Quotable Quotes" in the history of filmmaking. He says, "I believe God made me for a purpose, but he also made me fast. And when I run I feel His pleasure."

Isn't that a great line? God made me fast. "When I run I feel His pleasure."

Let me ask you something, a very personal question: When do you feel God's pleasure? When is it that you do something that makes God smile? What is it that God made you to do that when you do it, you just know that it pleases God because you can feel God's pleasure? What are those special moments in life that are so sacred and so powerful that you can feel the tingle of God's joyous presence and affirmation?

We are not the first to ask this question. For thousands of years, people have wondered about this question. The prophet Micah, way back in the eighth century B.C., asked it like this: "What does God really want from us? What can we bring to him that genuinely pleases him? Does God want burnt offerings or fragrant ritual oils or human sacrifices? No, no, no! All God wants is for us to do justice, to love kindness, and to walk humbly with our God. That's what pleases him" (Micah 6:6-8, paraphrased).

And that is helpful, but our scripture passage for this chapter is even more helpful. In Matthew 3:13-17, Jesus is ready to begin his ministry. He goes out to be baptized by John the Baptist in the Jordan River. Understandably, John is reluctant to baptize Jesus. John doesn't feel worthy to do that. Who would? John says, "You should be baptizing me." But Jesus convinces John to do it, and as Jesus is baptized, a voice from heaven says these powerful words: "This is my beloved Son, with whom I am well pleased" (Matthew 3:17 RSV). In these words, we find the best clue for how we can feel God's pleasure,

namely this: Become Christlike! God is pleased with us when we take on the spirit of Jesus. God is pleased with us when we live in a Christlike way. We can feel God's pleasure and sense his smile when we become, as the hymn-writer put it, "more like the Master."
Let's roll this out a bit with three thoughts.

First of All, We Feel God's Pleasure When We Forgive the Way Christ Forgave

This is one of the most dramatic messages of the Christian faith: *You are forgiven!* Now, pass that forgiveness on to others. Live daily in the Christlike spirit of forgiveness. How can we who have been forgiven so much because of Christ not be forgiving toward others? This was a dramatic theme in the teachings of Jesus Christ.

In the spring of 2005, we mourned the loss of Pope John Paul II, and the world reflected on the great things he had done in his life. He had done many great things, but to me, without question, the greatest thing he ever did occurred on December 27, 1983, when he went to Rebibbia Prison to forgive the man who had tried to kill him.

The picture was on the cover of *Time* magazine January 9, 1984. In a bare, white-walled cell in Rome's Rebibbia prison, Pope John Paul II tenderly held the hand that, two years before, had held the gun that was meant to assassinate him.

The photo was amazing. It showed
• two men shaking hands and embracing,
• two very different men from radically different worlds,
• one man young, the other older,
• one a Turkish Muslim, the other a Catholic Christian,
• one in a resplendent white robe, the other in the garb of a prisoner,
• one a beloved and respected world leader, the other a convicted criminal.

For twenty-one minutes, the Pope sat with his would-be assassin, Mehmet Ali Agca. The two talked softly. Once or twice, Agca laughed. The Pope had come to Agca's prison cell to forgive him for the shooting. At the end of the meeting, Agca either kissed the

27

Pope's ring or pressed the Pope's hand to his forehead in a Muslim gesture of respect, indicating that reconciliation had happened. Somewhere in heaven at that moment, God was smiling, and I'm sure that at that moment, Pope John Paul II could feel God's pleasure.

What Pope John Paul II did there in Rebibbia prison was profoundly Christian. In my opinion, it was the most Christlike thing he ever did.

• He sought out the enemy.
• He embraced the enemy.
• And he forgave him.

This event asks us, "Does forgiveness have a place in an age of violence and vengeance?" The answer to that question is indeed a resounding "Yes!" And that is the message Pope John Paul II was sending to the world: Forgiveness is better than vengeance. He learned that from Jesus.

But when will *we* ever learn?

We spend weary days and sleepless nights brooding over our resentments, calculating ways to get even, demanding our pound of flesh, seething over our grievances. We are shackled by our silly pride, unbending, unmerciful, unable, and unwilling to forgive and forget, and isn't that tragic? Because the truth is that revenge is never sweet; it ultimately becomes a sour stomach and a bitter memory and a poisoned soul.

Jesus knew this, and so he called for us to be bridge-builders, to be peacemakers, to receive forgiveness from him and offer it to others. This was a key theme of many of his parables. It was a dominant theme in the Sermon on the Mount. It was the major theme of his life. So this is number one: First of all, we feel God's pleasure when we forgive the way Christ forgave, when we offer to others Christlike forgiveness.

Second, We Feel God's Pleasure When We Include Others the Way Christ Included Others

Go, read the Gospels. You can't miss it: Christ's love is inclusive. He was constantly reaching out to the lowly, the lonely, and the outcast and bringing them into the circle. God wants us to be inclusive like that.

Have you heard about the all-American football player who came back to his alma mater as an assistant coach? One of his main responsibilities in his new job would be to recruit players for his college team. But before he made his first recruiting trip, he went in to visit with the head coach, the same coach for whom he had played some years before.

The head coach was a crusty old veteran. He had held that position as head coach for many years and was widely known and highly respected all across the country. The new young coach said to him, "Coach, I'm about to head out on my first recruiting trip, but before I go I want to be sure that we are on the same page. So what kind of player do you want me to recruit?" The crusty old head coach leaned back in his chair. He looked the young coach straight in the eyes and said, "I've been at this job a long time, and I have noticed that there are several different kinds of players. For example, you will find some players who get knocked down and stay down. That's not the kind we want! You will find some players who get knocked down, will get right back up, but they get knocked down again and then stay down. That's not the kind we want!"

And then the old coach said, "But you will also find some players who get knocked down and knocked down and knocked down, and each time they get knocked down, they get right back up!"

At this point, the young coach got excited and said, "Now that's the kind of player we want, isn't it, coach?"

"No," said the old head coach. "We want the one doing all that knocking down!"

That's what we need on our church team:

Players who will do some knocking down.

Players who will knock down not other people but walls that divide people!

Players who will knock down walls that separate and hurt and alienate and estrange.

We as Christians are called to knock down walls of hate and hostility and bigotry and prejudice and build bridges of love and acceptance and inclusion and reconciliation. This is what that powerful passage in Ephesians 2 is all about. It's one of the greatest passages in the entire Bible. Look at it: "For Christ Jesus is our peace, who has made us both one and has knocked down the dividing wall of hostility.... So then, we are no longer strangers or aliens but now are members of God's household with Christ Jesus himself as our cornerstone" (verses 14, 19-20, paraphrased).

It is interesting to note that the name of Jesus means "Savior" or "The Lord's Helper," but also notice (don't miss this now) that the name "Jesus" is the Greek form of the Hebrew name "Joshua." And we recall, of course, who Joshua was. Joshua was the one who with the help of God caused the walls to come tumbling down! Remember how the great spiritual sings it: "Joshua fit the battle of Jericho and the walls came tumbling down."

Let me ask you something: Are there walls in your life right now that need to be knocked down, walls that separate people, walls that divide people, walls that hurt and alienate and shun other people, walls that promote prejudice and hostility and distrust and bigotry? Jesus came to show us in words and in actions how inclusive God is and to remind us that there are no "walls" that separate in God's flock. All are valued. All are cherished. All are treasured. All are wanted. All are welcomed. All are included. That's the way God is, and that's the way God wants us to be. When the walls have been knocked down, somewhere in heaven God is smiling.

First, we feel God's pleasure when we forgive the way Christ forgave; and second, we feel God's pleasure when we include others the way Christ included others.

Third and Finally, We Feel God's Pleasure When We Love the Way Christ Loved

A few years ago I was at the airport to catch a flight for Columbus, where I was going to be guest-preaching. As I was checking my luggage at the check-in desk, suddenly the attendant said in a bright, happy voice, "Oh, you are a Special Selectee today, so you will need to go in to the main desk!" I thought, *Wow! A Special Selectee! That probably means a free ticket or an upgrade to First Class or a special prize.*

At the main desk inside, it happened again. The young woman at the desk said cheerily, "Oh, you are a Special Selectee today!" Finally, I said, "Thank you! What does that mean?" She replied, "It means you have been selected to have your luggage thoroughly screened today, so take your luggage over there." Oh, what joy to be a Special Selectee!

Well, right now, I want us to all be "*Christian* Selectees," because I want us to take a moment to carefully screen our "Love Luggage." How are we doing as a church and as individual Christians in receiving the love of Christ into our hearts and then passing that love on to others? It is so important that we be loving people! It is so crucial that we take seriously the command of Jesus to "love one another"— underscore the next five words—"*as I have loved you*" (John 13:34, emphasis added). This means that our love should be Christlike— gracious, generous, seeking, sacrificial, unconditional love.

In the time of Jesus, the people were taught to love, but they were taught to love only those who looked like them and dressed like them and talked like them and acted like them, and to see everybody else as enemies or adversaries or outcasts or sinners. But then here came Jesus, saying, "No, no, no! Your love circle is too small. Love *everybody,* even those who are different from you! Love all of them as I have loved you."

It is so vital, so urgent, that we be gracious, loving people. It matters more than I can tell you. Let me show you what I mean with a true story that touched my heart.

Some years ago, a young woman came to the church I was serving one Sunday morning. She was depressed and had been up all night brooding and crying and was seriously considering ending it all. But before she resorted to that, she decided to give the church one more chance. Earlier in her life, she had had a bad experience in another church that had left her bitter and disillusioned. She left that church in anger, vowing to never set foot in any church ever again for as long as she lived.

But now she was down to her last straw, so she showed up at our church that Sunday morning with, as she put it "a chip on her shoulder," thinking, "these people don't care about me; I bet nobody will even speak to me here in this big church." And then she met Dorothy!

When she walked into the church foyer, the first person she saw was Dorothy, but not before Dorothy saw her! Dorothy was one of those amazing people who just always graciously reached out with love to every person she met. Dorothy was one of those people who could not only light up the room but also could light up the lives of those around her. Dorothy rushed over to greet the troubled young woman and to welcome her to our church. Dorothy took the young woman under her wing, showed her around, and introduced her to everyone as "my new best friend." She took her to her Sunday School class and then to the eleven o'clock worship service and then out to lunch to Dorothy's favorite restaurant and continued to include her and compliment her and encourage her and introduce her to everybody they saw.

It was a remarkable experience for the young woman. She had never felt so loved!

She and Dorothy became best friends even though Dorothy was several years older. They sat in church together every Sunday. A few months later, the young woman came down to the altar at the end of the service and joined the church with Dorothy at her side. Dorothy was holding her hand and beaming!

Later, the young woman told me her story, about how she came to church that day not expecting much and planning to end it all that very afternoon and how Dorothy had welcomed her with open arms and loved her and saved her life. She said that now every time she hears the phrase *Christlike love*, she thinks of Dorothy.

At that moment somewhere in heaven, God was smiling.

Because you see, God made us Christians, and when we in the spirit of Christ forgive others and include others and love others that's when we can feel God's pleasure.

5

Why Can Christians Face Death Triumphantly?

O Death, Where Is Thy Victory?
O Grave, Where Is Thy Sting?

John 20:11-18

But Mary stood weeping outside the tomb. As she wept, she bent over to look into the tomb; and she saw two angels in white, sitting where the body of Jesus had been lying, one at the head and the other at the feet. They said to her, "Woman, why are you weeping?" She said to them, "They have taken away my Lord, and I do not know where they have laid him." When she had said this, she turned around and saw Jesus standing there, but she did not know that it was Jesus. Jesus said to her, "Woman, why are you weeping? Whom are you looking for?" Supposing him to be the gardener, she said to him, "Sir, if you have carried him away, tell me where you have laid him, and I will take him away." Jesus said to her, "Mary!" She turned and said to him in Hebrew, "Rabbouni!" (which means Teacher). Jesus said to her, "Do not hold on to me, because I have not yet ascended to the Father. But go to my brothers and say to them, 'I am ascending to my Father and your Father, to my God and your God.'" Mary Magdalene went and announced to the disciples, "I have seen the Lord"; and she told them that he had said these things to her.

I N DECEMBER OF 2003, A MOVIE CALLED *BIG FISH* WAS RELEASED. THE main character in the film, a man named Edward Bloom, loved to charm people with his larger-than-life stories (some would call them "tall tales") about his youthful and extraordinary adventures with circus performers, with giants and werewolves, and one amazing encounter with a so-called witch.

In the witch story (which was his son's favorite bedtime story), Edward Bloom describes in vivid detail how when he was ten years old, he and some of his young friends ventured into a swamp to check out a bizarre report they had heard. According to the story, a woman reputed to be a witch lived in this swamp, and if you could find her and look into her glass eye, you could see how you are going to die. With the bravado of ten-year-old boys, they decide to give it a try.

When they find her house in the swamp, the boys dare Edward to go and tell the woman that they want to see her eye. Edward goes and brings back the woman. She is old, has scraggly hair, and has a patch over her left eye. Only two boys are still there. The others have run off, terrified. The woman lifts her eye patch, and one of the boys sees himself as an old, old man falling off of a ladder. It scares the dickens out of him, and he and his brother run home in fear.

Now, only Edward remains. What should he do? Does he really want to look into her eye? Does he really want to know? On the one hand, knowing how you are going to die could "spook you out"; but on the other hand, you would know that you are going to survive everything else.

Edward decides to go for it. The movie does not reveal what Edward Bloom sees. Rather, the camera zooms in on his face as he smiles and says, "Huh. That's how I go?" This scene in the movie concludes with the grown-up Edward tucking his son into bed and saying, "From that moment on, I no longer feared death."

Every now and then, Easter comes along to remind us that as Christians, we don't have to fear death. Easter shows us dramatically and powerfully that we don't have to look into some woman's glass eye to see how we are going to die. Rather (and so much better), we can now look into the eyes of the resurrected Christ and see how, through faith in him, we can conquer death; how he has the power to deliver us from death. That's what Mary learned early on that first Easter Sunday morning.

Remember the story with me. On the Thursday night before Easter, Jesus was arrested on trumped-up charges. He was brutally beaten, rushed through a fixed trial that was held strangely in the middle of the night, and was declared guilty. The next day, Good Friday, Jesus was crucified, and he was buried in a borrowed grave. And then on Easter Sunday morning, Mary Magdalene came to the tomb to do what had to be done, to care for Jesus' dead body.

But when she arrived, she discovered that the stone that had been covering the opening to the grave had been rolled away. Mary looked inside. She was startled to see that Jesus' body was gone. She thought someone had broken into the grave and stolen the body. She was crushed, heartbroken, devastated. *They crucified him, and now they have taken his body away.* "How could they be so cruel?" she cried.

But then Mary heard a noise behind her. She turned and saw the silhouette of a man. She thought it was the gardener until he called her name. "Mary," he said tenderly. Mary recognized that voice, and at that moment she ran headlong into Easter. She realized the truth: It was Christ. His body had not been stolen. He had risen! He had conquered death! He had defeated evil! He had come back to life! He had been resurrected!

Mary had come to the tomb that Easter morning looking for a dead body but found instead a risen Lord. And with that discovery, Mary was resurrected too! No more weeping and wailing. No more heavy sighing. No more tears of sorrow. Christ sent her running and shouting the good news: "I have seen the Lord! He is alive! I have seen the Lord! He is risen!"

On that Easter Sunday morning long ago, the key moment came when the risen Lord called Mary by name, and she turned and looked into his eyes. Right now, at this moment, the risen Lord is still speaking, and if you will listen real closely you can hear him. Listen to that: he is calling your name and mine. Can you hear him? He is calling us by name and telling us that he has conquered death and that he wants to share with each one of us personally the good

FAITH IS THE ANSWER, BUT WHAT ARE THE QUESTIONS?

news of Easter, the good news of his great victory, the good news that goodness wins, that love wins, that God wins.

On that hill called Golgotha, evil had its best chance to defeat God and could not do it. God wins and wants to share that victory with you and me. That is the good news, the amazing news that can change our lives forever. Let me show you what I mean with three thoughts.

First of All, Because of Easter, We Can Be People of Hope

Do you remember the final scene from the Broadway musical *Camelot?* King Arthur sits alone in the forest. He is resting and brooding. He is totally disappointed and disillusioned. His whole world has come apart. His dream for Camelot has been shattered because he has been betrayed and is now at war with his former best friend and most trusted knight, Sir Lancelot. King Arthur's heart is broken.

But then suddenly, a young boy about twelve years of age finds him and tells King Arthur that he has come to join Camelot. He wants to help build this kingdom where honor and trust and respect and love and goodness and nobility prevail. He wants to be a Knight of the Round Table.

Suddenly, King Arthur realizes that his dream has not died. The vision of yet a court of justice and equality, a land of right and truth, a people of nobility and goodness and integrity, the vision—the dream—it's still alive.

The king quickly orders the boy to kneel. Taking his mighty sword, Excalibur, Arthur places the flat blade on each of the boy's shoulders, and then King Arthur says to him in a loud and proud voice, "I knight you Sir Tom of Warwick." And then King Arthur lifts the young boy up and says to him, in effect, "Go back home, my son. Tell everyone that Camelot is possible. Run, Sir Tom! Run! Tell the world it's still possible. Run, Sir Tom, run! Tell everyone that hope is still alive!"

What a moment! And that is what is happening here in the Easter story in John 20. Jesus is sending Mary out to the world with this message of good news.

Run, Mary, run!
Go find the others!
Run, Mary, run!
Tell them the news!
Run, Mary, run!
Tell everyone that I am still here!
Run, Mary, run!
*Tell the world that hope is still alive! That love is still alive! That goodness
is still alive! That God is still alive! Run, Mary, run!*

That's what Easter teaches us—that God is still in charge; that
God will win; that God is always with us; that God loves us; that when
we are down and out, God comes looking for us, and as he did with
Mary on that first Easter Sunday morning, he calls us by name. God
has the power to resurrect, the power to resurrect *us*. God has the
power to turn trudging to running, to turn sorrow to joy, to turn
tears of grief to tears of gratitude, and to turn death to life.

That's number one: because of Easter, we can be people of hope.

Second, Because of Easter, We Can Be People of Love

Love wins out over hate. Love endures. Love is the most powerful
thing in the world. That is the message of Easter.

Vic Pentz loves to tell a story about a minister friend's grandmother and her journey to America. Vic says that some years ago
when his friend's grandmother was a young teenaged girl in Austro-
Serbia, she found herself in a most difficult situation: She was being
beaten by her abusive father. Finally, she couldn't take it anymore,
so one day she ran away from home and caught a boat to America.

But when she arrived at Ellis Island in the New York Harbor, the
main port for immigrants entering the United States, she had no
papers, no family, and no sponsor. So as she stood in the long line,
the authorities, realizing that she had no credentials, put a white *X*
in chalk on her arm. This meant that when she arrived at the official desk of entry, she would be deported immediately.

As the official moved away to interview others, a young man next
to her in line reached over and wiped out the *X* on her arm. When
they arrived at the desk and the authorities asked for her papers, the

young man put his arm around her shoulder and said, "She's with me." Together, they were welcomed to America, and a few weeks later they were married! And later, their grandson, Vic's friend, became the pastor of a large Presbyterian church in Oklahoma (Victor D. Pentz, "Hallowed—Or Hollowed—Be Thy Name?" *The Protestant Hour,* 8/18/2002).

That young man's love saved that woman and granted her admission into a new life in a new land. And that is precisely what Jesus Christ does for us. With sacrificial love, he reaches over and wipes away the *X* on our sleeve and says, "She's with me. He's with me. This one's with me." Because of Jesus, we are not deported or cast out or pushed aside. Because of him, we are saved. Because of him and his love, we get to enter into a new life in a new land.

Now, there's another side to that coin: Christ is loving, and he wants us, his disciples, to be loving like him. He wants us to live daily in that Christlike spirit of love, caring, and compassion. He wants us to receive his sacrificial love and then to pass it on to others. He wants us to emulate his love in all of our relationships.

The point is clear: Because of Easter, we can be, first, people of hope; and second, people of love.

Third and Finally, Because of Easter, We Can Be People of Victory

On March 26, 2004, one of our doctors discovered that my wife, June, needed to have major surgery as soon as possible. The surgery was performed and went well, but more treatment was needed.

So over the next twelve months, we made more than sixty-eight trips to the medical center, and the treatments went very well. June is doing great, and she has been an inspiration to all of us who know her and to others with her spirit, her faith, and her courage.

Recently we went to see her doctor to get the results of her most recent tests. That is an intense experience. You sit in the small examining room and wait for the doctor and the results. Finally the doctor comes in. He speaks, asks about the children and grandchildren, and you visit a bit, and then he says, "May I have a moment?"

The doctor sits down at his computer and pulls up the test results. He stares at the screen and studies it intently. Then he pulls up another report and studies that with keen interest. Then to a hard copy, and then back to the screen, and you watch him. You watch his face, his expression, his body language. You watch for any sign, and you listen for any sound that will give you an advance signal for what is coming, because you know at any moment he will turn to you and say words that will impact your life incredibly.

Then, he turns and says, "Your CT scan looks good and stable, and the other test results are excellent. You are doing very well." And when he says that, you want to sing the Doxology and hug the doctor—in that order!

Now, let me hurry to say what we all know: Sometimes the news is not good. For all of us at some point in our life, the news will not be good. But even then, because of Easter, because of Jesus, because of God's promise to always be with us in this life and in the world to come, we can still be people of victory, because *nothing*, not even death, can separate us from God's love. In this life or in the next, God will give us the victory.

That is the message of Easter, the promise of Easter, the good news of Easter. "O death, where is thy victory? O grave, where is thy sting?" Thanks be to God, who gives us the victory through Jesus Christ, our Lord and Savior.

Because of Easter, we can be people of hope, people of love, and people of victory!

6

What Are the Dramatic Signs of a Healthy Faith?

Acts 2:1-4

When the day of Pentecost had come, they were all together in one place. And suddenly from heaven there came a sound like the rush of a violent wind, and it filled the entire house where they were sitting. Divided tongues, as of fire, appeared among them, and a tongue rested on each of them. All of them were filled with the Holy Spirit and began to speak in other languages, as the Spirit gave them ability.

LET ME BEGIN THIS CHAPTER WITH THREE QUICK STORIES. SEE IF YOU can find the common thread that runs through them.

The first story is about a woman who is a motivational speaker, and who often is asked to give the keynote address at conventions and convocations. Recently she returned home after speaking five nights in a row. Her husband said, "Honey, I know you must be really tired. Why don't you 'sleep in' in the morning?"

That sounded good to her, so she did stay in bed longer than usual. When she finally got up she put on an old worn-out blue robe that was frayed and faded but comfortable, and some old house shoes that had no back to them—the kind that you have to slide your foot into and then slide your foot as you walk to keep them on. Then, she walked past a mirror and saw that her hair was a major disaster, so she stopped and put some of those big pink plastic rollers in her hair. That done, she headed for the kitchen to start her day. When she walked into the kitchen to get her morning coffee, she noticed it immediately: Her husband had forgotten to take out the trash! In that community if you didn't get your trash out on time, it was tough luck. They would not wait for you. So she grabbed the two big trash bags quickly and began to shuffle outside, pulling the heavy trash bags along the ground, trying to keep her worn-out robe closed by holding her arms close together, sliding her feet along to keep her house shoes on, and sporting huge pink plastic rollers in her hair.

Just at that moment, the garbage truck was pulling away. She shouted to the driver: "Am I too late?" And the driver took one look at her and replied, "No, hop on!"

The second story comes from a minister friend of mine in California. When he first moved there, he played golf a couple of times with a man named Tom. Some months later, my friend's wife said, "You used to play golf with Tom, but you two haven't played together for some time now. Why don't you play golf with Tom anymore?"

He replied, "Well, would you play golf with somebody who kicked his ball out of the rough into the fairway, or who took a countless number of mulligans, or who hit the wrong ball, or who didn't write down the correct score on the score card, and kept hitting ball after ball into the lake?"

His wife replied, "No."

And he said, "Well, Tom wouldn't, either!"

The third story comes from a minister who put an ad in the local paper for a well-rounded handyman, someone who could fix things around the church and help out with routine chores. The very next morning after the ad ran, a well-dressed young man came and asked to speak to the minister. The pastor sized up the young man and then asked him a flurry of questions.

"Can you start a fire?"

"Yes, sir!"

"Can you have breakfast ready by seven o'clock every morning?"

"Yes, sir!"

"Can you polish the silver and wash the dishes?"

"Yes, sir!"

"Can you keep things picked up and neat, and the lawn mowed?"

"Yes, sir!"

And the minister continued, "And, of course, there will be electrical problems and unexpected leaking pipes and restroom overflows and ..."

"Wait a minute!" The young man interrupted. "I came here to make arrangements for my *wedding*. But if it's going to be like *that*, I think I'll just forget the whole thing!"

Now, all three of these stories are humorous. They made me laugh when I first heard them. But what is even better about them, and the thing that is the common thread that runs through them and links them together, is that we know these three stories the only way we could. The people telling these stories—the motivational speaker and the two pastors—are all telling the stories on *themselves*. They are laughing at themselves as they tell the stories, and they are doing so with obvious joy and delight.

That is a dramatic sign of a healthy person, to have a sense of humor and to be able to laugh at yourself. It's delightful to laugh with children at the cute and funny things they sometimes say. It's fun to laugh at the comical antics of circus clowns or the hilarious wit of good comedians. But the best humor of all is when we laugh at ourselves. It's a real mark of emotional maturity. It eases our self-pity; it diminishes our pride and saves us from taking ourselves too seriously. The famous actress Ethel Barrymore said it well, "You grow up the day you have your first real laugh at yourself." To have a good sense of humor, to be able to laugh at yourself, those are significant and dramatic signs of a healthy personality.

Now, let's take this a little deeper and ask this question: What are the dramatic signs of a healthy *faith*? Well, what do you think? If you were asked to make a list of the key signs of a healthy faith, what would you write down? To get into this, let's conduct a brief "faith checkup." What I would like to do is place before us a series of three test questions that will enable us to take our spiritual pulse, to evaluate our present spiritual temperature, to check our spiritual heartbeat.

Are you ready? Here is question number one.

First of All, Do You Have a Healthy Relationship with God?

Think about that. How is your relationship with God right now? Is it warm and wonderful, alive and well? Is it healthy or unhealthy?

Some people have a relationship with God based on fear and guilt. They say, "I had better shape up and obey the rules, or else God is going to get me." This is an unhealthy approach to faith because it makes God "the bogeyman," who is out to get us—and nothing could be further from the truth. According to the Scriptures, God is not "the bogeyman." Rather, God is our best friend, who is out to find us and save us and bring us safely back into his loving arms.

Other people have a relationship with God based on self-interest. They say, "I had better be good, so God will reward me and bless me now and let me go to heaven later." This too is an unhealthy approach to faith because it regards God as nothing more than an impersonal computer who automatically and mechanically rewards us when we do good and who punishes us when we do bad. According to the Bible, that is not the way God works at all.

Jesus showed us dramatically that God loves us graciously, generously, compassionately, sacrificially, and unconditionally. So God is not some unfeeling, uncaring, impersonal computer who does nothing more than react in kind to what we do. No, to the contrary, God is our living Lord, our personal Savior, who comes looking for us like loving parents searching desperately for their lost child, laying their lives on the line to find us and save us and reclaim us and to draw us back into their loving arms, where we belong.

We do good things not in order to get God to love us, but because God already loves us and we are so grateful we can't sit still. Relationships with God based on fear or guilt or self-interest are basically unhealthy. They are flawed from the get-go because, you see, a healthy relationship with God is based on trust. We do our best and trust God for the rest.

That's what Pentecost is all about. It's the celebration of the gift of the Holy Spirit. God is with us, and we can trust God; that is the promise of Pentecost. It is also the great promise of God recorded on page after page of the Bible. This is God's most significant promise: to never abandon us, to never leave us, to always be with us, to always be by our side, to give us the strength we need for whatever difficulty or challenge or obstacle we face in this world.

Author and speaker Nell Mohney was here not long ago to lead a women's conference. The women of the conference were kind enough to let me sit in on one of the sessions, and I'm so glad I did, because in that session, Nell Mohney told a story out of her own personal life that touched my heart.

Nell and her husband, Ralph, had two sons. Their younger son, Rick, was in a terrible traffic accident when he was twenty years old. For five days, the family members walked the floor of the hospital in Chattanooga, hoping and praying that Rick would make it, and for five days the doctors were encouraging. They thought he would pull through, but then things turned the other way, and tragically, Rick died. Just twenty years old, and he was gone.

Nell's husband, Ralph, was pastor of the largest United Methodist church in the city at the time, and when the memorial service was held on that next Sunday afternoon, the sanctuary was filled. The whole city was in grief. The following Sunday morning, Nell went to church all by herself. Her husband was in the pulpit, and her older son had gone back to his college out of town. Before the accident, Rick had been living at home and going to a local college. He had always gone to church with his mom, and he had always sat next to her. But now he was gone, and Nell went to church that morning all alone. She says that walking into church all by herself the Sunday morning after Rick's funeral was the hardest thing she had ever had to do in her life. Just before she entered the sanctuary, she prayed, *O God, please be with me. Please be with me. Please give me the strength I need to do this. O God, be with me.*

Nell walked in and sat in her usual place, and out of habit, she moved over and left a place open on the aisle, the place where Rick always sat. She looked at that empty spot, and it was almost unbearable; she felt so alone.

Just then, there was a movement beside her. Nell looked over to see a little nine-year-old girl slip into that seat. The little girl reached over and held Nell's hand, and all through the service, every now and then the little girl would pat Nell's hand and say, "I love you,

Mrs. Mohney. I love you, Mrs. Mohney." Nell Mohney said she had felt the presence of God with her many, many times in her life, and that morning, when she needed God more than ever, God was with her! God was with her in the presence and in the spirit and in the love and thoughtfulness of a little nine-year-old girl.

In telling that story, Nell Mohney showed us that she has a healthy relationship with God, a relationship built not on fear or guilt or self-interest, but rather on doing your best and trusting God for the rest.

That's also the kind of trust Simon Peter must have had when he stood up to preach on the first day of Pentecost. "O God, help me; O God, please be with me." God was with him. God's spirit blew on that place, and God gave Peter the right words to say and the courage to say them. And three thousand people were converted that day because Peter did his best and trusted God for the rest (see Acts 2:14-42).

Let me ask you something: Do you trust God like that? Do you have a healthy, wholesome, lively, vibrant relationship with God, built on trust?

Now, let's move to the second question.

Second, Do You Have a Healthy Relationship with Others?

Some years ago, two young men went camping in the Rocky Mountains. They were having a marvelous time until a ferocious snowstorm hit suddenly, placing them in great danger. They knew they had better get back to a nearby lodge, but the wind was howling, the air was frigid, and the snow was so intense that they could not see more than about a yard in front of them. They held hands and started trying to move to safety, but the going was so difficult that they got lost. It was a perilous situation. They were in danger of freezing to death. Hours and hours passed, and they still could not find their way. They were frightened and near panic, when suddenly they stumbled over something and fell to the ground. It was another camper. What should they do, leave the man there or try to save him? Their first thought was to leave the man there and fend for themselves, but they knew they could not do that. So they worked with the man, revived him, and together the three men put their arms around one another and continued to move together.

The going was slow at first, and they wondered if they would make it and even doubted that they could. More hours passed, and their hope was almost gone. But then they saw a light. Thank God. It was the lodge. And they knew then that they were saved!

The medical staff worked with them and told them that they had survived because they had held on to each other. Their togetherness had kept them going, and their shared body heat had kept them alive! They made it by holding on to each other. There is a sermon there somewhere!

This story shows why the church is so crucial: It gives us a community of faith to hold on to—people to keep us going. And on top of that, the Pentecost story reminds us that all of us in the world are family. On that Pentecost Day, all those people were drawn together. People from different nations, different cultures, different languages, and different backgrounds were all united that day by God's Holy Spirit. They communicated that day because of the presence and power of the Holy Spirit of God. The symbol that day was not a clenched fist to fight off, but an open hand to take hold of and celebrate.

Those campers only survived by holding on to each other. That's *our* calling too, isn't it? To see other people not as enemies or as adversaries to be destroyed, but as brothers and sisters to hold hands with. When will we ever learn this lesson?

Well, how is it with you? Do you have a healthy relationship with God built on trust in him? Do you have a healthy relationship with others built on love and respect?

Third and Finally, Do You Have a Healthy Relationship with Yourself?

More and more, we are learning how essential it is to have a wholesome self-esteem, a healthy love and respect for ourselves. If we feel good about ourselves, we are much more likely to become happy, productive persons who make this world a brighter and better place. On the other hand, those with poor self-esteem, those who don't like themselves, are much more likely to have problems and to *be* problems in the world.

Criminologists are discovering now that the vast majority of people who take up a life of crime, violence, and drugs are those with low self-esteem. Healthy self-esteem creates happy people. Poor self-esteem creates hostile people. If you find people who are always negative, always complaining, always unhappy, always criticizing their coworkers, you can be sure that they have a self-esteem problem. Their bitterness is within. They are unhappy with themselves. But there is help from God. Simon Peter's self-esteem had been shot when he denied his Lord three times. And even though Christ came and found him and forgave him, still Simon Peter's self-respect was not restored until the Holy Spirit came into him at Pentecost. After that, his confidence returned, and he gave all the credit to God.

When the Holy Spirit comes into our hearts, we can sing to God that prayer-hymn "You Raise Me Up," made famous by Josh Groban:

> You raise me up
> To more than I can be.

This powerful song reminds us that God's Holy Spirit can empower us to do things beyond our imagination and that we are strong beyond our imagining when we stand on God's shoulders. That's precisely what the Pentecost story is all about.

That's the way it works. When the breath of God breathes on us, it gives us a healthy relationship with God, a healthy relationship with others, and a healthy relationship with ourselves.

7

How Does Faith Help Us Rise Above Our Problems?

John 21:15-19

When they had finished breakfast, Jesus said to Simon Peter, "Simon son of John, do you love me more than these?" He said to him, "Yes, Lord; you know that I love you." Jesus said to him, "Feed my lambs." A second time he said to him, "Simon son of John, do you love me?" He said to him, "Yes, Lord; you know that I love you." Jesus said to him, "Tend my sheep." He said to him the third time, "Simon son of John, do you love me?" Peter felt hurt because he said to him the third time, "Do you love me?" And he said to him, "Lord, you know everything; you know that I love you." Jesus said to him, "Feed my sheep. Very truly, I tell you, when you were younger, you used to fasten your own belt and to go wherever you wished. But when you grow old, you will stretch out your hands, and someone else will fasten a belt around you and take you where you do not wish to go." (He said this to indicate the kind of death by which he would glorify God.) After this he said to him, "Follow me."

J UST AS I DID IN THE LAST CHAPTER, LET ME BEGIN THIS CHAPTER WITH three stories. See if you can find the thread that links them together.

First, have you heard about the couple who had been married for over sixty years? As they approached yet another anniversary, they both became nostalgic and reflective about their married life together. The husband said, "I have always wanted to ask you something. From the night we married, you have always had a box in your closet. I have never looked inside it. It's your private property, but I have always wondered what is in that box."

And the wife said, "Well, since we have been married for over sixty years, I think you are entitled to know. So if you'll go and get it, I will show you."

The husband brought the box to her, and when she opened it, he saw that it contained two crocheted doilies and $250,000 in cash. "Let me explain," the wife said. "The night before we married, my grandmother called me over to her house, and she said, 'Honey, I want you to have a long marriage, so I'm going to tell you how to accomplish that. Here is the key: Don't fuss with your husband. If you get upset with him, don't fuss with him. Just rise above it.' I asked her, 'But Gramma, how do you do that?' And Gramma said, 'Every time you get upset with your husband, don't fuss. Just go and crochet a doily.'"

Upon hearing this, the husband began to swell with pride, thinking *All these years, more than sixty years, and just* two *doilies.* "But," he said, "what about the money? What about the $250,000 in cash?"

And his wife replied, "That's the money I made from selling doilies!"

The second story is about a minister who serves a small church in the Midwest. To make his Easter sermon more dramatic, he decided to use three helium-filled balloons to illustrate the three points of his sermon.

His first point was that just as Christ arose and came out of the tomb, even so, by his power and grace, we can rise and come out of the tombs that imprison us. And at this moment in the sermon, the minister dramatically released the first balloon, and, gracefully, it rose up, floating to the ceiling.

His second point was that we now, as the present-day disciples of Jesus Christ endowed with his power and grace, can rise up and take up his ministry of love. Then the minister dramatically released the second balloon, and, gracefully, it rose up, floating to the ceiling.

His third point was that just as after Christ's death and resurrection,

Christ ascended into heaven, even so, when we die, because of his power and grace, our spirits will rise up and ascend into heaven. Then the minister dramatically released the third balloon, and—would you believe it?—that third balloon, as it drifted up toward heaven, got caught in the ceiling fan and began to go *whoosh, whoosh, whoosh*, round and round and round in what had to be a preacher's nightmare! But this preacher rose to the occasion that day, and he said, "As I have often told you, the journey to heaven is not easy. It has lots of twists and turns, and we can get knocked around quite a bit, and except for the grace of God, we would never make it!" And miraculously, amazingly, incredibly at that precise moment somehow, that third balloon got released from that fan, and it floated gracefully up to the ceiling. Then the minister said, "Let us pray." And he prayed, perhaps a little more fervently, *"Thank you, Lord! Amen."*

The third story is about a young man who took a job in a large grocery store. On his first day on the job, a woman came up to him and asked him if she could buy half of a grapefruit. The young man didn't know, but he told her that he would find out. So he took the grapefruit and walked through the supermarket, through the meat department, through the stockroom, into the manager's office at the back of the store, and he said to the manager, "Sir, I'm sorry to bother you, but some silly woman wants to buy half of a grapefruit."

Just at that moment, the young man sensed the presence of someone behind him. He turned to see that the woman had followed him through the store, through the meat department, through the stockroom, and into the manager's office, and she had heard him say, "Some silly woman wants to buy half of a grapefruit." But quickly, that young man rose to the occasion, and he said, "and *this* nice lady wants to buy the *other* half!" They sold her the half grapefruit, and she went happily on her way.

As the young man turned to go back to work, the manager stopped him and said, "Son, I know what happened here. You got yourself into a jam. But you worked out of it beautifully. You rose to the occasion. I like that! That impresses me. By the way, where are you from?"

The young man answered, "Lancaster, Pennsylvania. You've probably never heard of it. It's famous for its great hockey teams and its boring women."

51

"That's interesting," said the manager. "My *wife* is from Lancaster, Pennsylvania."

Thinking quickly, the young man said, "Which team did she play for?"

Now, *that's* what you call "rising to the occasion"! And that, of course, is the theme running like a thread through all three of these stories.

Another expression we use frequently in everyday conversation that relates to this is "rise above it!" With God's help, rise above your problems, your heartaches, your disappointments. By the grace of God and through the power of God, we can rise above the dark prisons that try to enslave us. This is a dramatic part of the Easter message. Christ was resurrected, and so were his followers. He arose out of the tomb; so did they, and by the power and the grace of God, so can we!

Let me show you what I mean.

First of All, We Can Rise Above Despair

By the miracle of God's grace, we can come out of that grave called despair. In the Easter story, Mary Magdalene is the dramatic symbol of that victory. Think about it. She came trudging to the tomb on Easter morning, weeping, filled with despair, the picture of gloom and sadness. She was brokenhearted because she had lost someone she loved (see John 20:11-18).

We can all relate to that, can't we? We have all walked through the grief valley. No experience in life is more universal than that. Someone close to Mary had died, and she was devastated. We all know the feeling. George Bernard Shaw reportedly once said, "Death is the ultimate statistic ... one out of one of us dies," but that doesn't make it any easier. As the poet William Wordsworth put it, speaking poignantly about the death of his good friend Lucy, "she is in her grave, and, oh, / The difference to me!" ("She Dwelt Among the Untrodden Ways," ca. 1799).

One of the most beloved entertainers of all time was the comedian George Burns. He died in Beverly Hills on March 9, 1996. He was 100 years old. When he was in his nineties he wrote a book entitled *How to Live to Be 100 ... or More.* In the book he has a chapter with the heading "Stay Away from Funerals, Especially Yours." George Burns noted that some of his friends look in the obituary column in the morning and if their names aren't there, they go ahead and have breakfast. He said that if he ever looked in the obituary column and found his name was there, he would go ahead and have breakfast anyway, because, he said, "I'm not leaving on an empty stomach" (George Burns, *How to Live to Be 100 ... or More* [New York: G. P. Putnam's Sons, 1983], 157).

Now, that kind of sense of humor kept George Burns young at heart for all of his 100 years. But the fact is that we are all going to die, and even more painful is the fact that people we love are going to die, and that can fill us with despair. Like a heavy blanket, despair can cover us over and smother the very life out of us. Like a dark and somber tomb, despair can enslave and imprison us and choke off our vitality. That's what Mary felt that morning as she trudged to the tomb—despair.

But that's not the end of the story. She came looking for a dead body, but instead she found a risen Lord; and when Mary saw the resurrected Christ, she got resurrected too. No more trudging. No more heavy sighs. No more weeping and wailing. She burst out of the tomb of despair running and shouting, "I have seen the Lord! He is risen!"

In his book *Growing Deep in the Christian Life* (Grand Rapids, Mich.: Zondervan, 1986), Chuck Swindoll tells of a Christian school's kindergarten teacher who wanted to gauge her new students' level of religious training. She found a little five-year-old boy who knew absolutely nothing about the story of Jesus. The teacher began by telling the boy about the death of Jesus on the cross. When he asked her what a cross was, she created a makeshift cross with some sticks and told him that Jesus was nailed to a cross, and then he died. The little boy looked down and quietly said, "Oh, that's too bad." Quickly though, the teacher told the boy that Christ rose again and came back to life. Hearing that, the little boy's eyes grew big, and he exclaimed, "Totally awesome!"

Well, it *is* totally awesome, when you stop to think about it. The "place of the skull," where Jesus was crucified, has become a throne.

Knowing that, we are still going to hurt when someone we love dies. But knowing that, with the help of God, we, like Mary Magdalene, can rise above despair!

Second, We Can Rise Above Disillusionment

By the miracle of God's grace, we can come out of that tomb called disillusionment. In the Easter story, Cleopas and Simon on the Emmaus Road are dramatic symbols of that victory, the triumph over disillusionment.

Disillusionment is the problem that occurs when people try something that doesn't quite live up to their expectations. They feel let down and then turn with a real sense of disappointment, a real sense of betrayal, even a real sense sometimes of bitterness. They accepted the promises. They tried, and yet somehow, they feel it didn't come through for them. They took the spiritual check to the bank, it bounced, and they became disillusioned!

That's the picture we see in Cleopas and Simon as they trudge sorrowfully down the Emmaus Road. It is Easter afternoon. They know about the Crucifixion, but they have not yet encountered the Resurrection. Disappointed, disillusioned, heartbroken, hopeless, they have just given up: "We thought Jesus was the one to save us. We should have known this wouldn't work. It was all too good to be true, too idealistic for this cruel world, and now it's all over." That is the graphic portrait of disillusionment.

But look what happens. That is not the end of the story. The risen Lord comes to them and walks with them and resurrects them too! He brings them out of the tomb of disillusionment, and they get back with the other followers—in other words, they get back in church!

Disillusionment, we all know about that, don't we? The problems of the world weigh heavily upon us and tempt us to give up. For example, have you heard the one concerning a man about to be rescued after he had spent a long time shipwrecked on a tiny deserted island in the South Pacific? The sailor in charge of the rescue team stepped onto the beach and handed the man a stack of newspapers. "Compliments of the captain," the sailor said. "The captain would like you to glance at the headlines to see if you'd still like to be rescued!"

Sometimes the headlines do scare us. Sometimes it feels as though evil is winning. But then along comes Easter to remind us that there is no grave deep enough, no seal imposing enough, no stone heavy enough, no evil strong enough to keep Christ in the grave. This is the good news of the Christian faith: God wins! Knowing that, we will still have our dark moments; but knowing that, with the help of God, we, like Cleopas and Simon, can rise above disillusionment!

Third and Finally, We Can Rise Above Defeat

By the miracle of God's grace, we can come out of that tomb called defeat. In the Easter story, Simon Peter is the dramatic symbol of that victory.

Simon Peter had been so brash, so confident, so cocky, but then at "crunch-time," he failed: he denied his Lord. He was so ashamed and so defeated! But the risen Lord came and resurrected him. He gave Simon Peter another chance.

"Simon, do you love me?"

"Oh yes, Lord, you know I love you."

"Then feed my sheep!"

The risen Lord was saying to Simon Peter, "Don't quit on me now. You have a job to do. You are not defeated. You can bounce back. You fell down, but you can get up. You can rise above it! Don't quit on me. I'll be with you. I will help you."

There's a beautiful story (likely an urban legend) that speaks to this. According to the legend, Ignace Paderewski, who rose to prominence as Poland's most famous pianist and prime minister, once scheduled a concert in a small, out-of-the-way village in hopes of cultivating the arts in rural Poland. A young mother, wishing to encourage her son's progress at the piano, bought tickets for the Paderewski performance. When the night of the performance arrived, the woman and her young son found their seats near the front of the concert hall and eyed the majestic Steinway piano waiting onstage. Without thinking, the mother found a friend and began visiting and talking with her, and in the excitement of the evening, the little boy slipped out of sight!

When eight o'clock arrived, the house lights came down, the spotlights came up, the audience quieted, and only then did anyone notice the little ten-year-old boy seated at the concert piano, innocently picking out "Twinkle, Twinkle, Little Star." The boy's mother gasped, and the stagehands started out to grab the boy. But suddenly, Paderewski appeared onstage and waved them away.

Paderewski quickly moved to the piano, and standing behind the little boy, whispered into his ear, "Don't quit. Keep playing! Don't stop!" Leaning over, Paderewski reached down with his left hand and began filling in a bass part. Soon his right arm reached around the other side of the boy, encircling the child, to add a running obbligato. Together, the old master and the young novice held the crowd mesmerized with great music in a magical moment.

Nothing transforms life more than having the strong voice of the Master, who forever surrounds us with love, whispering in our ear time and time again, "Don't quit! Don't stop! Keep on playing!" But not only does our Master encourage us to continue in our novice ways, God also weaves into our work magnificent obbligatos and supplements our melody with gloriously beautiful harmony.

What is created then is enhanced by the touch of the Master's hand. When the risen Lord said to Simon Peter, "If you love me, feed my sheep!" he was saying to Peter and to us, "Don't stop! Keep playing! I want to share my resurrection with you! Don't quit on me now." He was saying that with God's help, we can rise above despair, we can rise above disillusionment, and we can rise above defeat.

8

Did Jesus Really Mean It When He Said, "Love One Another"?

Luke 7:36-50; John 15:12

One of the Pharisees asked Jesus to eat with him, and he went into the Pharisee's house and took his place at the table. And a woman in the city, who was a sinner, having learned that he was eating in the Pharisee's house, brought an alabaster jar of ointment. She stood behind him at his feet, weeping, and began to bathe his feet with her tears and to dry them with her hair. Then she continued kissing his feet and anointing them with the ointment. Now when the Pharisee who had invited him saw it, he said to himself, "If this man were a prophet, he would have known who and what kind of woman this is who is touching him—that she is a sinner." Jesus spoke up and said to him, "Simon, I have something to say to you." "Teacher," he replied, "speak." "A certain creditor had two debtors; one owed five hundred denarii, and the other fifty. When they could not pay, he canceled the debts for both of them. Now which of them will love him more?" Simon answered, "I suppose the one for whom he canceled the greater debt." And Jesus said to him, "You have judged rightly." Then turning toward the woman, he said to Simon, "Do you see this woman? I entered your house; you gave me no water for my feet, but she has bathed my feet with her tears and dried them with her hair. You gave me no kiss, but from the time I came in she has not stopped kissing my feet. You did not anoint my head with oil, but she has anointed my feet with ointment. Therefore, I tell you, her sins, which were many, have been forgiven; hence she has shown great love. But the one to whom little is forgiven, loves little." Then he said to her, "Your sins are forgiven." But those who were at the table with him began to say among themselves, "Who is this who even forgives sins?" And he said to the woman, "Your faith has saved you; go in peace."

"This is my commandment, that you love one another as I have loved you."

AMAN WAS DRIVING HOME FROM WORK ONE DAY WHEN HE SAW A GROUP of young children selling lemonade on a corner near his home. The kids had posted the typical sign over their lemonade stand:

Lemonade—10 cents

The man was impressed with these enterprising young children, so he pulled over to the curb to buy a cup of lemonade and to give his support to the children's financial effort.

A young boy approached the man's car. The man placed his order for one cup of lemonade, and he gave the boy a quarter. After much deliberation, the children determined that the man had some change coming, and they rummaged through their cigar-box cash register and finally came up with the correct amount.

The boy returned with the change and with the man's cup of lemonade. The boy then just stood there by the man's car and stared at the man as he enjoyed his fresh lemonade. Finally, the boy asked the man if he were finished. "Just about," the man said. "But why?"

The little boy answered, "That's the only cup we *have,* and we need it *back* to stay in *business!*" It's difficult to operate a lemonade business if you have only one cup!

But you know, this story is something of a parable for what Jesus saw in the religious leaders of his day. When it came to love, they had only one cup. They taught people to love, but it was a very restricted, lim-ited, narrow, conditional love that they lived out themselves and that they called for from their followers. "Love those who look like you and act like you and dress like you and talk like you and eat like you and think like you, and shun everybody else. Love only those we have admitted into our inner circle, and see everybody else as the enemy, the adversary, the outcast." When it came to love, that was the only cup they had.

But then along came Jesus with a different idea and a different approach. Jesus loved everybody. He accepted everybody. He included everybody. He reached out graciously and intentionally to those who were down on their luck and to those who were hurting, to those who were poor and needy, to those who were in trouble, to those who were sick or afflicted, to those who were labeled as outcasts; and tenderly, he drew them into the circle of love. When it came to love, Jesus had lots of cups to share. And then Jesus said to his followers, "Look now, this is the way I want you to love: love one another as I have loved you." Take up the torch of Christlike love!

This was so important to Jesus, but the truth is, at first the disciples did not get it. They were not tuned in! What Jesus was calling on them to do was a dramatic departure from that "we only have one cup" approach to love that they had been taught all of their lives— to love only those who are just like you and, for sure, not to love those who are outsiders or outcasts. But then here came Jesus, saying, "No, no, no. Don't be like that anymore! Rather, use a 'multi-cup' approach. Reach out to everybody you meet with love and grace and respect and acceptance and tenderness!"

Now, with that in mind, look at this little scenario that someone wrote with lots of imagination about what could have taken place when Jesus met with his disciples in the Upper Room the night before he was crucified, to give them their final instructions. This make-believe scenario goes like this.

> Jesus said to them, "I give you a new commandment. Love one another and everyone you meet as I have loved you. By this love, all will know that you are my disciples."
> Simon Peter said, "Do we have to write this down?"
> And Andrew said, "Will this be on the next test?"
> And James said, "Does *spelling* count?"
> And Philip said, "Do we have to know it word for word?"
> And Matthew said, "When do we get out of here?"
> And John said, "Does this apply to all of us?"
> And Thomas said, "I doubt that this will work."

And Judas said, "What does this have to do with real life?"
And Jesus wept!

The creator of this scenario is reminding us that sometimes, like the early disciples, we are not as tuned in to Jesus as we should be. But look at the context of this. Jesus said these words in the Upper Room the night before the Crucifixion. These were his final instructions to his followers, and the concise message here is not just to love, but to love in a Christlike way. That is our calling as Christians: to love others as Christ has loved us—graciously, generously, sacrificially, unconditionally.

That is precisely what this story in Luke 7:36-50 is all about. Remember it with me. A Pharisee invites Jesus to his home as the guest of honor at a banquet. But strangely, the Pharisee does not treat Jesus like a guest of honor. Normally, three courtesies were extended to the respected guest. First, the host would give his guest the kiss of peace. Second, cool water would be poured over the guest's feet, to cleanse and comfort them. And third, the guest's head was anointed with a pinch of sweet-smelling incense or perfume from rose petals. When Jesus arrived in the Pharisee's house, none of these things was done.

Why? Maybe the Pharisee has a hidden agenda. Maybe he has invited Jesus there to try to trip him up or trap him with loaded questions over dinner. Maybe he doesn't want to appear too friendly with this itinerant preacher from Nazareth, this one his colleagues were wondering about and worried about. Or maybe the Pharisee is afraid of "guilt by association" because he knows that Jesus has just been out in the streets associating with some outcasts of society, tax collectors and sinners. Whatever the case, the Pharisee does not perform these three acts of good manners and respect.

In those days, houses of well-to-do people were built around an open courtyard in the form of a hollow square, and often, the banquets took place in the courtyard. People passing by on the nearby street could easily look in or walk in so that they could listen to the lessons given by Pharisees and rabbis as they ate together and discussed theology and lessons of faith over their meal. A woman in the crowd, a woman who—how shall I put this?—has a reputation around town, is there from off the street. She is listening and watching, and she notices that good manners have not been expressed to Jesus, so she rises to the occasion! First, she washes Jesus' feet with her tears. Second, she dries his feet with her hair. And third, she anoints his feet with her perfume. The Pharisee is highly offended. He is shocked that Jesus would let this woman of the streets even touch him. But Jesus sees it as a beautiful, tender, thoughtful, loving gesture, and he commends her, includes her, and forgives her.

Now, there are many fascinating elements in this story, but for now let me just lift up one question for us to think about, namely, this: What was it about Jesus that drew people to him?

What was it about Jesus that caused the regular, ordinary people of the streets like you and me, and even the outcasts, to resonate with him?

What was it about Jesus that attracted the masses to him?

Why did they come from far and near just to get a glimpse of him?

What was Jesus' authority?

Why did the people crowd the roadsides to see him and the mountainsides to hear him?

Why did people who had leprosy and people who were blind and people who were sick seek him out?

Why did the outcasts of that society, such as this woman in Luke 7, feel wanted and welcomed and valued and loved and accepted in Jesus' presence?

Well, there are many reasons why. Let me list just three ideas about this for our consideration. I'm sure you will think of others, but for now, let's try these three on for size together, because they show us how the love of Christ, the love he commands us to emulate, is indeed a "multi-cup" approach and a many-splendored thing.

First of All, People Were Drawn to Jesus Because He Brought Them Good News

You see, people, then and now, were starving for some good news. Religion, for many of the people, had become cold, staid, authoritarian, negative, prohibitive, irrelevant, fearsome, and sometimes even abusive and exploitive. The religion of their time did not speak to their hurts. It did not bring them joy. That's why they were so drawn to Jesus, because he brought them good news. Over and again, Jesus said to them, "You count! You matter! Fear not! Don't be afraid! God loves you! God is with you!"

Let me make the point with a parable written by Dr. Fred Craddock. One evening a farmer named John was heading for home, and he was running late. He tried to take a shortcut across an unfamiliar field. But he fell into an old, abandoned cistern, a deep, deep hole. He was a proud and strong man, so he said, "I can get out of here." John was knee-deep in mud and sand, however. He reached to the sides of the cistern, mossy green and slick and wet, but he had no leverage. He could not get out. Finally he swallowed his pride and cried out, "Help, help!"

A neighbor walking by heard his cry and looked down in there and said, "John, is that you? I can't believe you are down there! Look at you down there in that ugly hole—an embarrassment to your family, an embarrassment to yourself. You are a disgrace!" The neighbor really told him off. Then the neighbor went on into town and told everybody about it and how he had told John off. The neighbor said, "I've been wanting to say that for years!" It was quite a speech, but John was still in the hole. John continued to cry out for help—more desperately now.

Next, a couple of politicians came by and saw John's plight, and they were upset. They said, "This is awful! This should have been taken care of years ago!" So they went into town; got the city council together; passed a law; and then came out and put up a sign that read, "Twenty-five dollar fine to fall into this hole." And it was a good law, they said—"It needed to be passed."

John was still in the hole, however. John cried out louder, "Help, help, help!" Some people driving by heard his cries. They looked down into the hole and said, "This is a disgrace to our community. We can't have this." So they notified the beautification committee, and they came out and planted some azaleas and dogwoods and yellow roses. It was beautiful, but John was still down in the hole.

Now, with raspy voice and almost no hope left, John called out, "Please, somebody, help me! Help!" Just about then a man came by, and he looked down there and saw John in this awful fix. He had compassion in him, and he said, "Let me help you. I can get you out. Here, take 'hold of my hand." And in that moment, the only thing important in John's world was that hand (From a lecture series presented by Dr. Fred Craddock at First United Methodist Church in Longview, Texas).

Do you know who that was? Do you know whose hand it was that pulled John out of that hole? Of course you do. Most of us recognize that hand, and most of us remember how he pulled us up and out and saved us. That is the good news of our faith, isn't it? Others may scoff at us or fuss at us or ignore us, but Christ wants to get on with the saving!

In the powerful movie *The Hiding Place,* Corrie ten Boom (magnificently portrayed by our dear friend Jeannette Clift George) says this: "There is no pit so deep that God's love is not deeper still!" That is why people were drawn to Jesus: he brought them good news, the good news of salvation and love and acceptance.

Second, People Were Drawn to Jesus Because He Practiced What He Preached

In Mark 12, Jesus talks about hypocrisy, exposing it for what it is:

> Beware of the scribes, who like to walk around in long robes, and to be greeted with respect in the marketplaces, and to have the best seats in the synagogues and places of honor at banquets! They devour widows' houses and for the sake of appearance say long prayers. They will receive the greater condemnation. (vv. 38-40)

The people were drawn to Jesus because they were fed up with hypocrisy, and they knew he was no hypocrite. He meant what he said. He practiced what he preached. He saw faith as a style of living. He was authentic, genuine; and the people sensed it, felt it, knew it.

A few years ago I was on a preaching mission in another city. One evening during the worship service, a high-school-age girl gave a magnificent devotional talk. She spoke of love as the key sign and symbol of the Christian faith. She encouraged us to be thoughtful, considerate, and kind. She finished her comments with a beautiful paraphrase of 1 Corinthians 13, known as the love chapter. All of us were impressed. The congregation was visibly moved. But after the service I heard this same young girl, who had just spoken so powerfully on the importance of love, talking to her mother in the church parking lot. Her mother had been five minutes late picking her up, and the girl was upset because she would miss five minutes of a television program. She spoke to her mother in a cruel, vicious tone. She called her mother "stupid," "clueless," an "old fool," an "idiot," and another profane name that I will not repeat. She was arrogant, haughty, rude, and hostile, the very opposite of what she had proclaimed so eloquently in the sanctuary only moments before. I felt so sad, so let down, because we want people to practice what they preach.

People were drawn to Jesus because he brought them good news, and because he practiced what he preached.

Third and Finally, People Were Drawn to Jesus Because to Him, They Were Not Outcasts

To Jesus, they were not outsiders, they were not untouchables; they were special! Each was unique. Each was valued and treasured. Each was a child of God to be loved and respected. Jesus did not see them as second-rate. He did not shun them as outcasts, as though they were beneath him. He did not abuse them or exploit them or ignore them. He did not look down his nose at them. That is why the regular folks, the people of the streets, the masses, the sick and the lowly, the outcasts gravitated to Jesus. To him, they were *not* lowly; they were *not* common; they were *not* despised; they were *not* outcasts. Jesus made them feel valuable, important, cherished, cared for, accepted, and loved. And as Christians, that is what Jesus wants us to do as well.

Let me conclude this chapter with one of my all-time favorite stories. It's about a woman in Birmingham who, on a cold winter's morning, saw a little boy standing on the grating just outside of a bakery. It was snowing and sleeting, and the little boy was barefooted and had no coat, just a tattered T-shirt and some worn-out blue jeans. He was trying to warm himself with the air coming up from the vents of the grating.

The woman's heart went out to the little boy. She couldn't stand seeing him shivering in the cold. "Where are your shoes and coat?" she asked him. When he told her that he didn't have shoes or a coat, she took him by the hand, and they went to a nearby department store. The woman bought the little boy a nice coat, and some socks and shoes and gloves. The boy was so proud! He thanked her and thanked her, and then he asked her a surprising question. He said, "Lady, are you God's wife?" The woman was embarrassed by this question at first, but then she replied, "No, I'm not God's wife, but I *am* one of his children." The little boy grinned and said, "I *knew* it! I *knew* it! I just *knew* you were some kin to him!"

Let me ask you something: Can people tell by the way you live and by the way you love that you are kin to God? Jesus said, "Love one another as I have loved you. By this love, all will know that you are my disciples" (John 13:35; 15:12, paraphrased).

9

What in the World Are We Supposed to Do as Christians?

Matthew 28:16-20

Now the eleven disciples went to Galilee, to the mountain to which Jesus had directed them. When they saw him, they worshiped him; but some doubted. And Jesus came and said to them, "All authority in heaven and on earth has been given to me. Go therefore and make disciples of all nations, baptizing them in the name of the Father and of the Son and of the Holy Spirit, and teaching them to obey everything that I have commanded you. And remember, I am with you always, to the end of the age."

HAVE YOU HEARD THE STORY ABOUT THE YOUNG POLICE OFFICER who was on the witness stand testifying in the trial of a man he had arrested for robbery? The defendant was represented by a hard-nosed attorney, known far and wide for being tough on police officers. In cross-examination, the tough lawyer was trying to undermine the policeman's credibility, and the exchange between the fiery lawyer and the young policeman went like this.

The lawyer speaks first. "Officer, did you see, with your own eyes, my client committing this crime?"

"No, sir, I didn't see him, but my partner did."

"Well, if you didn't see him commit the crime, why did you arrest him?"

"Because my partner entered in the front of the store and I came in the back. My partner saw him taking money out of the safe, and when the defendant tried to run away, my partner pointed and shouted, 'There he goes!' I chased him, tackled him, and arrested him."

"And you trust your partner *that much*? You would just act on his word?"

"Yes, sir, I would trust him, and all of my fellow officers, with my life."

At this point, the tough lawyer smiled, because he thought he knew now just how to trip up the young policeman. He said, "With your *life*? Well, then, let me ask you this, officer: Do you have a room at the station where you change your clothes in preparation for your daily duties?"

"Yes, sir, we do."

"And do you have a *locker* in that room?"

"Yes, sir, I do."

"And do you have a *lock* on that locker?"

"Yes, sir."

"Do you lock your locker *every day*?"

"Yes, sir."

"Now, why is it, officer, if you trust your fellow officers with your life, that you find it necessary to lock your locker in a room you share with these same officers?" Again the tough lawyer smiled smugly because he felt he had trapped the young policeman.

But the young officer rose to the occasion, and he gave the perfect answer. He said, "You see, sir, we share this building with the legal court complex, and sometimes *lawyers* walk through that room!" The courtroom erupted in laughter, and a prompt recess was called. And it is said that the young police officer has been nominated for the "Comeback of the Year" award!

Well, when we read the Scriptures closely, we find ourselves wanting to nominate the early disciples of Jesus for the "Comeback of History" award. Just think of it.

When Jesus was arrested, the disciples got scared and ran away. When Jesus was crucified, they were down for the count—devastated, disillusioned, defeated. They were afraid, disappointed beyond words, confused, hurt, and heartsick. They had not counted on this at all, and they didn't know what on earth to do.

"What in the world do we do now?" That was their question, and they simply did not know how to answer that. They didn't have a clue. But then their hope was rekindled. Their direction was clarified. Their dream was still alive because their Lord was still alive! Jesus Christ came out of the tomb. He rose from the dead, and the risen Christ appeared to them numerous times.

One of those Resurrection appearances is found in Matthew 28. Jesus met his disciples back where it all started, in Galilee, and he gave them what we now call the Great Commission. Jesus said, "Go therefore and make disciples of all nations, baptizing them in the name of the Father and of the Son and of the Holy Spirit, and teaching them to obey everything that I have commanded you. And remember, I am with you always, to the end of the age" (vv. 19-20). The disciples knew then what they were supposed to do in the world, and a short time later, the Holy Spirit came and gave them the strength and courage and power to do it (see Acts 2). With the right answer in their minds and the Holy Spirit in their hearts, they went out and turned the world upside down—or, better put, right side up!

Now, let me ask you something. If a new Christian came to you today and said, "I have just become a Christian. I have accepted Jesus Christ as my Lord and Savior. *Now* what do I do? How do I relate to the world? What in the world am I supposed to do?" how would you answer that question? How are you answering it right now by the way you live? *What in the world are we supposed to do as Christians?*

This is a key question because it impacts every single thing we do as individual Christians and as a church family. Over the years and to the present moment, people have answered this question in three very different ways. Let's take a look at these three options and see where we fit in.

First of All, Some Say, "Reject the World"

"Escape from the world, run away, bail out, leave it." The idea here is that the world is evil, with all of its temptations and entice-ments and pressures, and the body is weak; so according to this view, the only hope is to flee, to forsake the world, to reject it.

There are many dramatic illustrations of this in history. For example, consider the monastic movement. As early as the fourth century, Christian monks by the thousands began running away from the world. They went to caves in the hills, to old tombs in deserted graveyards, and to the waste places of the desert. They thought they had a better chance for salvation by doing two things: first, by leaving the sinful world; and second, by weakening their bodies so that they would not have the strength to give in to the world's temptation. So they would run away to lonely, isolated, desolate places, and then they would punish their bodies. They ate as little as possible. They went for months, even years, without bathing. They slept in uncomfortable positions. They wore only enough clothing for decency. And they avoided all contact with persons of the opposite sex.

One of the most famous and colorful of these monks was Simeon Stylites. He retreated from the world by sitting on top of a series of columns, the tallest and final of these being nearly fifty feet high. The top of that column was only a yard wide. He stayed there for thirty-seven years and never came down once; food was sent up to him by a rope. When Simeon Stylites left the world, he really left! Later monks realized that this kind of rejection of the world was not productive, and they began to live together in groups so that they could do helpful, creative things such as running hospitals, orphanages, or schools.

Another dramatic example of world-rejection is seen in those religious groups who constantly emphasize the Second Coming of Christ, to the neglect of everything else. All that matters, they say, is to escape this world.

For example, in America in the 1800s, a religious leader from Vermont named William Miller announced that Christ would be returning to earth in the year 1844. Some of Miller's followers got carried away and even announced the exact day and time.

As that particular day and time approached, the tension mounted. Farmers stopped farming. Children dropped out of school. Merchants gave away their goods because soon there would be no need for them. The night passed, then the next day, and then the next night. Heartbroken, Miller's followers returned to the homes they had neglected and to crops that had remained unharvested.

Sadly, in recent years, we have seen tragic examples of this world-rejection approach: Jim Jones's Jonestown, where over 900 people died in a mass suicide in November of 1978; David Koresh's Branch Davidians tragedy in Waco, Texas, in April of 1993; and the Heaven's Gate group in San Diego in March of 1997, where nearly forty followers took their lives trying to escape this world.

A sweeter illustration of this "Reject the World" approach is seen in the Amish people. Please don't misunderstand me: I love the Amish people. I am not being critical of them. They are wonderful people from whom we could learn much, but the basic premise of their lifestyle is world-rejection.

Practices and customs may vary from one community to another, but in many ways, they reject the modern world. Often they will choose not to use automobiles or electricity. Many use hooks and eyes to fasten their clothes instead of buttons or zippers. They may choose to worship in private homes. They often prefer to have their own schools and feel that their children will be contaminated by contact with persons outside their group. Women wear the dress of a century ago. Men wear broad-brimmed hats and often do not shave their beards after they are married. They travel in horse-drawn buggies and wagons. They keep to themselves, to protect their way of life and to avoid the temptations of our modern times. Sweetly, but dramatically, they reject the world.

Beyond the Amish community, we also see this world-rejection idea on a personal level. Some people cannot handle the stresses, demands, problems, and suffering of the world, so they become neurotic or paranoid. Others withdraw to live hermitlike existences. And sadly, still others just choose to "end it all."

How do we relate to the world? Some say, "Reject it!" But there is a problem with this approach: It is not the biblical answer. It is not God's answer. When God created the world, he looked upon it and said, "It is good." Later, we are told, "God so loved the world that he gave his only Son" to save the world (John 3:16).

This brings us to the second approach. First, some say, "Reject the world."

Second, Others Say, "Resemble the World"

"Identify with the world"; "Blend in"; "Just go along"; "Be a thermometer"; "Don't rock the boat"; "Just register the climate"; "Embrace the world"; "Adjust to it"; "Don't worry about the Ten Commandments or the standards of Jesus Christ," they say. "Just accommodate yourself to the standards of the world. Don't stir the waters; just go with the flow."

Bishop Arthur Moore once told about a college student who became a Christian and joined the church in the spring of the year. Shortly after, this student went up north to work in a logging camp for the summer. His friends at church were worried about him, this new Christian, being exposed to the tough life of a logging camp. They were afraid the rough, worldly lumberjacks might tease him harshly or even persecute him because of his faith or tempt him to shortcut his best self. The young man's church friends prayed for him daily.

When the summer ended and he returned home, his friends at church quizzed him: "Did you make it all right?" "Was it difficult?" "Did the lumberjacks give you a hard time because of your faith?" He answered, "I made it just fine. No problems at all. I handled it well; they never found out that I'm a Christian!"

Let me ask you something: Can people tell that you are a Christian? Do you stand out in a crowd because the spirit of Christ is radiant in you? Or do you just blend in?

How should we relate to the world? Some say, "Resemble it!" But there is a problem with this approach: It is not the biblical answer; it is not God's answer. The scriptures tell us to not conform to the world, but rather to be the conscience of society, the light of the world, the salt of the earth, the leaven in the loaf.

Some say, "Reject the world." Others say, "Resemble the world."

Third and Finally, Still Others Say, "Redeem the World"

Change it! Improve it! Make a difference! Make the world a better place! Redeem it!

In 1986, Bob Brenly, the catcher for the San Francisco Giants, tied a Major League record with four errors in one game while filling in at third base against the Atlanta Braves. But then, in his last at bat in the ninth inning, with the count full at three balls and two strikes, Bob Brenly hit a home run and won the game for his team, 7 to 6. He went from goat to hero with one swing of the bat!

After that, the television announcer said, "Well, folks, Bob Brenly just redeemed himself." He *redeemed* himself! What does that mean? It means this: He changed things! He improved things! He delivered against all odds! He converted a bad situation into a good situation! He got a new life, another chance. He turned defeat into victory! But let me hurry to say that there are some situations that we can't redeem by ourselves. We need an outside source of strength to come and help us, to come and save us. This is what the Christ-event is all about.

Christ comes as an outside source of strength to redeem us, to deliver us, to save us, to give us a new life and another chance, and to give us a job! He puts us to work as his missionaries. He passes the torch to us. He sends us out as his representatives. He sends us out to be ministers of redemption for a needy, broken world. He sends us out to make disciples of all nations, to continue his ministry, to take to the world his caring, loving, healing, helping, redemptive touch.

Recently I ran across the story of the good Samaritan, as Jesus did not tell it. In this version, the Samaritan sees a man lying beside the road, half-dead, and the following conversation takes place.

Samaritan: What happened to you?

Man: I was beaten and robbed. Will you help me?

Samaritan: Let me give you some advice, my friend: Never travel this road alone again.

Man: Will you help me?

Samaritan [*to himself*]: I know I ought to do something to help this poor wretch. But after all, I'm from another district, and I didn't tell him to come this way. He should have known it was dangerous. He really has only himself to blame. But, still, here he is. I guess I must do what I can. So, when I get back to Samaria, I will write a letter to the authorities. I will write letters to the editor. I will get a group together, and we will think about what should be done.

73

Man: Will you help me?

Samaritan: Yes, I am going to help you. I must be off now to get my group together to talk about the problem.

Then, as the Samaritan walks away, he says to himself: *But first, I must finish my vacation in Jericho. Then, there are those sheep I want to buy. Well, I hope someone will come along to help that poor man. I am so busy. If he only knew, I'm sure he would understand. He should have stayed home, anyway.*

Aren't we glad that Jesus didn't tell the parable like that? He didn't tell the story like that because he wants us to be "little redeemers," to give our time, our energy, our prayers, our talent, our resources, our hands, and our hearts to redeeming the world, and he will always go with us.

Where there is a problem, with the help of God, we can solve it.

Where there is a wrong, with the help of God, we can right it.

Where there are hungry people, with the help of God, we can feed them.

Where there is no hospital, with the help of God, we can build one.

This is our task, our calling, our Great Commission.

Some years ago, a group of Christian athletes from America went on a mission work trip to Korea. After the group's project was completed, they were saying good-bye to the Korean villagers. Deep friendships had been established. It was a touching moment. Then, in the name of the host village, a little Korean girl brought flowers to the athletes, and, struggling with her English, she said, "These flowers will fade and die, but you will smell here forever!"

Well, I hope *we* "smell forever," here, there, and all over the world. My hope and prayer is that we will share the fragrance of Christ everywhere because our commission is not to reject the world or to resemble the world. Our job is, with the help of God, to redeem the world.

10

When Is Losing Your Baggage a Good Thing?

Hebrews 12:1-2
Therefore, since we are surrounded by so great a cloud of witnesses, let us also lay aside every weight and the sin that clings so closely, and let us run with perseverance the race that is set before us, looking to Jesus the pioneer and perfecter of our faith, who for the sake of the joy that set before him endured the cross, disregarding its shame, and has taken his seat at the right hand of the throne of God.

SOME YEARS AGO WE TOOK A GROUP FROM OUR CHURCH ON A TOUR OF the Holy Land. We were there for ten days, and it was wonderful. We had an amazing tour guide. A great Bible scholar and a respected archaeologist, he lives in Jerusalem six months of each year, so he knows the land, the languages, the customs, and the culture incredibly well. All of that put together gives him keen insights into the teachings of Jesus and the truth of the Bible. On top of all that, he never gets tired. He is like the Energizer Bunny—he just keeps going and going and going. That pretty much summarizes the daily schedule we had in those ten days in the Holy Land. We kept going and going and going, and it was a wonderful, once-in-a-lifetime experience.

But when we got on the plane to come home, we realized how

tired we were. It was a long flight back to Houston. Some people in our group fell asleep immediately, but I'm not one of those people who just doesn't sleep well on planes; I don't sleep *at all* on planes! So when we began to circle Houston, preparing to land, I looked out the window with tired eyes. What a thrill it was to see the Houston skyline, and then I saw our church, and my house, and I was so glad to be home. The trip was fantastic, but in my travel weariness, it felt so good to be back in Houston. And I couldn't wait to land and get my baggage and go home.

Finally, the plane touched down. It was a smooth landing, and, as often happens when a plane lands safely back home after a long flight from abroad, everybody on board cheered.

We got off the plane just fine, right on time. We made it through customs with no problem. Then we went to the luggage area to claim our bags. Just as we arrived, the buzzer sounded, the light came on, and the baggage carousel began to move. Quickly the people in our group began to pull their baggage off the carousel. Each member of our group in turn hugged me good-bye and scurried out to head for their homes.

Finally, I was the only one left. I stood there alone, watching the carousel move, looking intently with tired eyes for my luggage. By now, just a few lonely bags were left circling on the belt, and not one of them was mine. I stood there, waiting, watching, and hoping. And then with a sickening thud, the carousel stopped, and in that moment I realized that my baggage was lost!

Have you ever lost your baggage? It's an awful, frustrating, and helpless experience. Now, the good news is that the airline found my luggage and delivered it to our front door the very next day. But at that moment, as I stood there tired and anxious to get home, it was, to say the least, not one of the pleasant occasions in my life. My mind darted back to a sign I saw outside the airport in the Holy Land, which read: *May God and your baggage go with you.* And I thought, *Well, God did come with me, but my baggage did not.* And then I remembered another sign I had seen near the airport in Copenhagen: *We send your baggage in all direction*s. Well, I had made it back to Houston, but my baggage was who-knows-where. I felt deflated, discouraged, and defeated. That's what losing your baggage can do to you.

However, if you stop and think about it, there is a flip side to that coin, namely this: There is some baggage that we carry around with us all the time that we need to lose, that God *wants* us to lose. There is problematic baggage in our personalities that can hurt us and hurt other people, baggage such as prejudice, resentment, bitterness, jealousy, envy—baggage that hinders us and burdens us and robs us of the joy of life.

We actually have brought that concept into our everyday language. We say things like this: "He's good and talented, but he brings lots of baggage with him." "She's bright and capable, but before we hire her, we need to understand that there's a lot of baggage there." One NFL coach, talking about one of his star players at the end of last season, said, "He is a great player. He was probably the best athlete on our team, but we traded him because we just could not handle his disruptive antics and his selfish arrogance any longer. We never knew what he was going to do or say. He just became such a distraction that we had to trade him. We just could not handle his baggage anymore."

Some years ago, there was a very talented basketball player in the National Basketball Association. At first glance, he seems like a coach's dream: Tall, agile, strong, a great rebounder, a quick jumper—while the other players are gathering themselves to jump, he's already up and has the ball. He's not a ball hog—defense and rebounding are more rewarding to him—and he is absolutely tireless. Well, that player, with all those great athletic capabilities, performed well for a few seasons, but pretty soon he was out of basketball because he "self-destructed." He just had so much troublesome baggage in his personality that before long, no team wanted him.

Baggage problems can hurt us, and they *can* and *do* hurt other people. Look at these quotes:

"He is so talented, but he has a drinking problem."

"She is so brilliant, but she can't get along with anybody."

"He has great skills, but he has a terrible temper."

The point is clear: All of us have great things about us, but we also can carry around troublesome baggage that is harmful and destructive, and it burdens and encumbers us and everyone around us. *That* baggage, we need to lose. We need to lose it with the help of God.

This is precisely what our text in Hebrews 12 is talking about. Look again at these words: "Therefore, since we are surrounded by so great a cloud of witnesses, let us also lay aside every weight and sin that clings so closely, and let us run with perseverance the race that is set before us, looking to Jesus the pioneer and perfecter of our faith" (vv. 1-2a). Jesus is our hope. He is our Redeemer. He is our Savior. He is the One who can deliver us from the dangerous and destructive baggage that burdens and encumbers us.

Now, let me ask you something. How much troublesome baggage are you carrying around right now? How many bags do you need to lose, and what are they? What is it in your life that needs to be laid aside? Let me suggest three possibilities.

First of All, We Need to Lose the Baggage of Closed-Mindedness

With the help of Christ, we need to lose that bag, because closed-mindedness is so dangerous and so destructive. It is one of the things most responsible for nailing Jesus to a cross. They said, "We will not listen to what he is saying. In fact, we'd better silence him. Let's get him crucified." This kind of negative, closed-minded attitude is still with us. "I'm right, and I know it. Don't confuse me with the facts." That's the mantra of the closed-minded person.

Some time ago, Mayor Bill White came to speak to our group of Methodist Men. The mayor was asked how the SAFEClear program was going. This was a new program to move stalled cars off the roadway, to make our streets safer, and to keep the traffic moving. There had been a lot of discussion about it on television, in the papers, in the city council chambers, and over coffee cups and water coolers all over the city. Some people liked it, and some had problems with it. I don't know how everyone personally felt about the program, but I do know this: The mayor is a good man, and he was trying to do good things. He was trying to listen and respond creatively, but he said that the hardest part of his job was trying to deal with people who don't have the facts straight and who will not listen because their minds are closed.

To illustrate his point, the mayor told a true story about a little girl who was recently riding in the car with her father, and she said,

"Daddy, do you know about the SAFEClear program?" The father responded, "Well, I know a little bit about it. Do you know what it is?" "Oh, yes," said the little girl, "I know all about it. I know everything there is to know about it!" "Really?" said the father. "Tell me about it." "Well," the little girl said, "Here's how it works. If your car stalls on the road, they come and get it in six minutes, and then they take it to Mayor White, and he destroys it!"

Now, that kind of misinformed certainty is cute in a little girl, but it is not so pretty in grown-ups, and yet it is a negative, hurtful attitude that runs rampant in our world today. Nothing is more frustrating than trying to talk to a closed-minded person.

Sometimes a person will say to me, "I don't want to scare you, but I have a lot of questions about faith." That doesn't scare me at all. What scares me is the person who thinks he has all the answers. He won't listen to anyone else's point of view. That's the "scary" guy because he carries with him everywhere the baggage of the closed mind.

In the *Peanuts* comic strip, Violet is the epitome of the closed-minded person. She will not listen to anybody, and she thinks she is always right. One day she gets upset with Charlie Brown. She is ranting and raving and shaking her fist at poor old Charlie Brown. Finally, Charlie Brown says, "Now, if we, as children, can't solve what are relatively minor problems, how can we expect to..." And then, *POW!* Violet slugs Charlie Brown and says, "I had to hit him quick... He was beginning to make sense!"

That's what closed-minded people do. That's what the closed-minded people of the first century did to Jesus—they hit him quick with a cross because he was beginning to make sense.

Closed-mindedness is so dangerous and so destructive. With God's help and by his power, we need to lay it aside. That's one piece of baggage we do not need in our lives.

Second, We Need to Lose the Baggage of Arrogant Pride

Now, of course we all know that there is a *good* kind of pride. It's good to be proud of our church and our nation and our city and our children, and especially our grandchildren. But that's not the kind of pride Jesus warned us about. Over and over, Jesus warned us about haughty, pompous, arrogant pride; the holier-than-thou pride; the pride that shouts to the world, "I'm better than you!"; the pride that is conceited, pretentious, and puffed up. That kind of pride can poison our souls.

Her name was Miss Bessie. She was the town gossip and the self-appointed watchdog of everybody in town, always sticking her nose into other people's business and repeatedly starting vicious rumors about people. She did this constantly to remind people that she was "holier" than everybody. The townspeople didn't like this, but they were afraid that if they said anything, Miss Bessie might start a terrible rumor about them.

But one day she made a mistake that came back to haunt her. A new man named George moved to town. The first week he was there he went downtown to the bank. However, the only available parking spot was directly in front of the small town's only bar. George parked his pickup truck there, and he then went across the street to the bank and then to the hardware store. Miss Bessie walked by, saw George's truck in front of the bar, and immediately she began (in holier-than-thou, prideful tones) to tell everybody to watch out for George because he was an alcoholic. She herself had seen with her own eyes his red pickup parked in front of the bar in the middle of the afternoon. And that *proves*, without question, that he has a drinking problem.

The rumor got back to George, and he asked Miss Bessie about it. George told her that actually he's a teetotaler and doesn't drink at all and that he had never set foot in that bar. Miss Bessie stared at him with a self-righteous, haughty expression and said, "*Likely* story, *likely* story! Where there is *smoke*, there is *fire*, young man!" With that, she put her nose in the air and proudly marched away. George said nothing more; but later that evening, he just quietly parked his red pickup truck in front of Miss Bessie's house, and he left it there all night!

There's a sermon there somewhere, and I think it's the message that Jesus conveyed strongly in his teachings that arrogant pride is dangerous and destructive. It hurts us, and it hurts other people. With the help of God, we need to lay it aside.

Closed-mindedness and arrogant pride are two pieces of baggage we need to lose. We do not need them in our lives.

Third and Finally, We Need to Lose the Baggage of Ingratitude

We proclaimed 2005 to be "The Year of Grateful Celebration" in our church. That year, we celebrated our sixtieth birthday as a church. It was a good time to remember how much God had blessed us. Sometimes in the rush of things and in our hectic pace of life these days, we forget how indebted we are to God, and we begin to take all the credit.

Have you heard the story about the scientist who prayed to God one day, and he said, "God, we don't need you anymore. Science has finally figured out a way to create life out of nothing—in other words, we can now do what you did in the beginning."

"Oh, is that so? Tell me about it," God said.

"Well," said the scientist, "we can take dirt and form it into your likeness, then breathe life into it, thus creating man."

"Well, that's very interesting," said God. "Show me." Then the scientist bent down to the ground, gathered a handful of earth, and started to mold the soil into the shape of a man.

"Wait, wait, wait," God said to him. "You need to get your *own* dirt!"

Everything we have comes from the gracious hand of God, so ingratitude is not a pretty picture. With the help of God, we need to lay aside closed-mindedness, arrogant pride, and ingratitude. These are three pieces of baggage we need to lose. We do not need them in our lives. But the only way we can lose them, the only way we can set them aside, is by looking to Jesus. He is our hope, our Deliverer, our Savior.

11

How Do We Make Love Last?

John 13:34-35
"I give you a new commandment, that you love one another. Just as I have loved you, you also should love one another. By this everyone will know that you are my disciples, if you have love for one another."

A YOUNG HUSBAND WAS RUSHING OUT OF THE DOOR TO HEAD FOR HIS office early one morning. His wife said to him, "Do you remember what today is?" "Absolutely, I do," the husband said, quick as a flash. "And before this day is over, you will realize how well I know what today is, and how important it is to us as a couple." Of course, the truth is, he didn't have a clue!

When the man got into his car, he quickly called his secretary and told her that his wife had asked him if he remembered what special day this was. He confessed to his secretary that he had no idea, so could she help him figure it out? The young husband knew that it wasn't their anniversary. It wasn't her birthday, or his. It wasn't Valentine's Day. He was stumped. He could not figure it out. All morning long, he and his secretary discussed and researched this, but no luck; they could not come up with the answer.

So the husband decided to be proactive, hoping that as the day unfolded, he might be able to remember what special day it was. To be safe, he bought his wife that new dress she had been admiring at her favorite store, and he had it beautifully wrapped and sent out to their home. He also sent perfume and jewelry and flowers. He then made reservations at the best restaurant in the city, and he bought tickets for the new musical in town. Then he called his wife to tell her everything he had done to help them celebrate this special day in their lives appropriately. Still, she gave him no hint or clue.

The man left work early and rushed home. His wife met him at the door, looking radiant in her new dress and jewelry, and off they went for a festive night. The restaurant was superb. The musical was outstanding, and they had a wonderful evening.

When they arrived back home, the husband was so proud of himself and how well he had come through, but he still had no idea what day it was or what on earth they had been celebrating. So finally, he said, "Well, I hope you enjoyed our special day." And his wife said, "Oh, honey, I did! I did! This has been without question *by far* the greatest Groundhog Day we have ever had!"

I like that story because it reminds us that marriage can be fun and supportive and wonderful, and it can also be challenging! *Challenging?* Yes! If we have questions about that, all we have to do is go and take a look at the marriage statistics.

Look at how many marriages start out so well with great dreams and high hopes, but then, something goes wrong. Communication breaks down; affection grows cold; mistrust creeps in; and what started out as love is now replaced with indifference or complacency or even hostility. And you wonder, what went wrong? How did something so positive and so beautiful and so promising turn so negative and so painful? How did something so right go so wrong? Why didn't it last?

Now, let me hurry to say what we all know that some situations become so hurtful and so destructive, and sometimes even so dangerous, that the only answer is to dissolve the relationship, to learn from that and move on, and to make a new beginning with your life. And if that happens, you can know that God loves you and God is with you, and that the church is here with incredible resources to support you and encourage you and to help you shape a new beginning.

Apart from those hurtful situations, though, it is doable. Love can last and endure and grow and mature and flourish. Recently in our church family, we had 122 couples who had been married for fifty years or longer. Of these 122 couples, twenty-two couples had been married for more than sixty years. The point is that it can be done! How do we make love last? That is the crucial and key question we need to examine. Well, how do you do that? How do you keep the marriage on track? How do you keep the courtship alive? How do you keep the relationship vital and fresh and exciting and fulfilling and well? How do you make love last?

Let me list three thoughts about that. I'm sure you will think of others, but for now, think with me about these three ideas on how to make love last.

First of All, Love Each Other in a Respectful Way

To love each other with respect—in other words, with graciousness, with thoughtfulness, with kindness; that is so incredibly important. To respect the viewpoint, the personality, the ideas, the dignity of the other person is absolutely crucial.

Have you heard the story about the woman who arrived at the airport several hours before her scheduled flight? She went into the gift shop to buy a book to read while she waited. She selected a book, and then she saw something she could not resist: a large bag of chocolate chip cookies. She loved chocolate chip cookies, so she bought the largest bag they had, took the cookies and her new book in hand, found a seat in the waiting area at the gate for her flight, sat down, and became engrossed in her new book.

Some time passed, and then she heard a noise to her right. A man seated next to her was opening the bag of chocolate chip cookies on the seat in between them. The woman was so upset. Why, *the nerve* of that man, opening her bag of cookies and then—can you believe it?—he reached in and pulled out a cookie and began to munch on it. She was so irritated that she wanted to punch out this rude cookie thief! But she didn't want to make a scene, so she just reached over with an "I'll show him" attitude and pulled out a cookie for herself. The man smiled and reached over and took another cookie for himself. Irked even more by his selfish behavior, she grabbed another cookie, and the "cookie battle royal" was underway!

He would take a cookie out of the bag, and then defiantly, *she* would take one. On and on it went, until he pulled out the last cookie. He broke it in half and offered her one of the pieces. She snatched it and popped it into her mouth just as he did the same with his half. The woman was absolutely livid and was about ready to tell him off. But then she heard her flight called. In a huff, she gathered her belongings and headed to her gate. She refused to look back at this arrogant, rude man who had devoured half of her beloved chocolate chip cookies, this thieving ingrate who had not even had the courtesy to say *thank you* to her.

Relieved to be away from this awful man, she boarded her plane. Just as the plane took off, she reached into her carry-on bag to get her book. And she could not believe what she saw: there, before her very eyes, was her own unopened bag of chocolate chip cookies! With a sickening thud, she realized what had happened. *She* was the rude one! *She* was the ingrate! *She* was the thief! *She* was the one taking cookies that did not belong to her, and it was too late to go back and apologize!

The point is clear: Sometimes when we are absolutely convinced that we are right, we may be wrong! Sometimes when we think somebody else is totally at fault, the fault may be ours. Sometimes when we just *know* that something is a certain way, we may discover later that what we believed to be true was not! So keep an open mind and an open heart, because you just never know: you might be eating someone else's cookies. So, always, always be respectful. If you want love to last, be respectful.

Some years ago, a man came to see me. He and his wife were having marriage problems. The man said to me, "Aw, Jim, I know I'm rough on her. I know I'm critical of her. Sure, I fuss at her all the time, and I do have a hot temper. But she knows I don't mean it. She knows that's just the way I am, and she can take it." I had to tell him, "No, she can't take it. She comes to the church crying every week and saying, 'How can he love me when he talks to me like that?'"

It always astounds me in the counseling room to hear married people who supposedly love each other speak to each other in words and in body language with such disdain and contempt and disrespect. You can't build or sustain a marriage on that, so this is number one: if you want to make your love endure and flourish and last, then, first of all, remember to love each other in a respectful way.

Second, Love Each Other in an Understanding Way

Some years ago I heard Bishop Bob Goodrich speak at a ministers' retreat. He told a story that day that changed my life, a story that changed the way I look at other people. It underscores one of the greatest relationship principles I have ever heard.

The story was about a stern, strict English schoolmaster who lived in earlier days and who ran his one-room schoolhouse with an iron hand. "To spare the rod is to spoil the child" was his motto. He was hard and tough and demanding, a harsh disciplinarian. In that classroom, he was the law, and *his* way was the *only* way. The students obeyed him, or else they would suffer the hard consequences.

One day a new student moved to town and joined the class at midterm. He took his seat at the back of the room. The schoolmaster decided to make an example out of this new student, to show him and to remind all the others in the classroom that he was the absolute authority in that school and that he must be obeyed without question. So he said to the new student, "Young man, you are new here, so let me explain how we do things in this classroom. I make the rules, and *you* obey them! When I call on you to recite, I want you to stand to the left side of your desk, say your name loudly, hold your textbook in your right hand, and then recite." "But, sir," said the student. "Don't you question me!" the schoolmaster fired back. "You just do as I say!"

Later that day, the schoolmaster called on the new student. He stood to the left side of his desk as he had been told to do, he said his name loudly as instructed, but he held his textbook in his left hand instead of the right. This infuriated the teacher. He thought the young man was defying him, and in anger, the schoolmaster ran to the student, shouting, "Don't you disobey me! I told you to hold your textbook in your *right* hand!" Then the schoolmaster grabbed the young student, shook him harshly, and shoved him back down into his desk seat. As the student fell back, an empty sleeve swung around, revealing that the young boy had no right arm!

The point is clear and obvious, and so important to remember:

everybody has an "empty sleeve," and more often than not, we can't see it, and we don't know about it. It's so tempting to be harsh with other people when they don't act just the way we want them to act or do just what we want them to do. It's so easy to be critical of others and to find fault and point the finger. But the truth is, everybody has an empty sleeve of some kind, and if we know that, it's easier to accept other people, to respect them, to embrace them, to celebrate them, to forgive them, and to understand them.

Now, I have lots of "empty sleeves." Let me tell you about one of them. I can get claustrophobic, and so when I go to a theater or a movie or a conference or a ball game, I like to sit in the aisle seat. My wife June knows that. Our children know that, and they understand it. So they don't fuss at me or criticize me or tease me or try to change me. They just quietly and unobtrusively arrange things so I can sit on the aisle, because they know that's an "empty sleeve" for me, and they understand.

First, if you want to make love last, then love each other in a respectful way; and second, love each other in an understanding way.

Third and Finally, Love Each Other in a Christlike Way

That's what this amazing text in John 13:34 is all about. Jesus says to the disciples and to us, "A new commandment I give to you, that you love one another; even as I have loved you" (RSV).

Notice now that Jesus did not just say to "love one another." He said to love one another *as I have loved you.* Those last five words are the key words here: *as I have loved you.* This is the key to a great Christian marriage: two people loving each other with Christlike love, which, of course, means loving generously, graciously, compassionately, sacrificially, and unconditionally. That's the way to make love endure and flourish and last. That's the way to make a marriage work and be joyful and fun and celebrative—to love each other with a Christlike spirit, with a Christlike love; to love each other with the kind of love Jesus has for you and me.

Let me tell you about the one of the first weddings I performed as a minister. My wife, June, and I had been married just a few months. We were still in college, and I was serving a couple of small churches out in rural Tennessee. A young couple in one of those churches wanted to get married. They both came from poor farming families. At the wedding, the groom wore bibbed overalls, and the bride wore a dress her mother had made from material that had once been bags for holding flour.

June knew that they would not be able to afford a wedding photographer, so she brought along our little Kodak camera and made their wedding pictures. The reception was in one of the Sunday school classrooms there in the church. Some members of the church brought cookies and punch.

During the reception the groom asked me if he could speak to me in private. We walked outside to his pickup truck. He seemed shy and embarrassed, and then he said, "My dad told me I should pay you for performing our wedding, but I don't have any money." I said, "You don't need to pay me. I'm your pastor. It was a privilege for me to perform your wedding." And the young man said, "I would be dishonored if I didn't give you something, so I brought this." Then he reached into the back of his truck and pulled out an old brown, rumpled paper sack and handed it to me. I thanked him, and he hugged me. In the sack were six small green apples. That's all he had, and it was one of the most moving gifts I have ever received in my life.

Now, fast-forward thirty-five years. I was speaking at a church in Tennessee. After the service, I was visiting with the people when I saw a couple coming toward me, smiling. "Do you remember us?" the man said. "Help me a little," I responded. They said, "We were the couple you married—and look at us now. We have been happily married for thirty-five years because of something you told us." "What did I tell you?" I asked. They said, "You told us to communicate, to keep the courtship alive, to have a sense of humor, to be kind, and most important of all, to love each other in a Christlike way, and that's exactly what we have tried to do." Then the man said, "I gave up farming. I'm a carpenter now, and we still don't have much money, but we are so happy. Our home is full of love."

How do you make love last? By loving each other in a respectful way, by loving each other in an understanding way, and, most of all, by loving each other in a Christlike way.

12

How Does the Christian Faith Affect Our Attitudes?

Philippians 3:12-16
Not that I have already obtained this or have already reached the goal; but I press on to make it my own, because Christ Jesus has made me his own. Beloved, I do not consider that I have made it my own; but this one thing I do: forgetting what lies behind and straining forward to what lies ahead, I press on toward the goal for the prize of the heavenly call of God in Christ Jesus. Let those of us then who are mature be of the same mind; and if you think differently about anything, this too God will reveal to you. Only let us hold fast to what we have attained.

We have a young couple in our church family who are outstanding in every way. Both the husband and the wife are highly successful business executives. They are devoted to each other, devoted to the church, and devoted to their two beautiful daughters.

Their daily schedule is hectic, to say the least, and Saturday morning is the only time they have to sleep in. So they have a house rule that the children can get up early on Saturday morning to play if they want to, but they are not to come to their parents' bedroom before 7:00 AM.

Early in December, the couple's five-year-old daughter, Bailey, came into her parents' room at 6:00 AM. "Bailey, why are you in here so early?" her parents asked. "It's 6:00 AM, and you know the rule that you are not to come in here before 7:00!" As only a five-year-old little girl could do it, Bailey put her hands on her hips and said, "Duh! I can't tell time!" I'm not sure, but I think Bailey received a digital clock for Christmas!

This true story raises an important question for us to think about in this chapter: Can we tell time? Can we tell that it's time to leave some things behind us? Can we tell that there may be no time like the present to take a fresh look at our attitudes?

Some years ago, a superstar basketball player was recruited by a local university. He showed up on campus with lots of fanfare and lots of press clippings. National television covered his first game, and this true freshman lived up to his advance billing, and then some. He dominated the game and led his team to victory.

All went well until the post-game interview. On national television, the young player started "talking trash." Now, trash talking is a relatively new fad in sports that I hope will soon fade away. In general, the trash talker spouts off brashly about how great he is and about how he is going to destroy the opposition.

Now, while this freshman basketball player was doing this trash talking during his first time on national TV, the telephone suddenly rang in the background. Someone came over and interrupted the interview to tell the freshman that his mother was on the phone, calling long-distance. The young man took the call, and on national television, his mother said, "Son, you played a great game, and I'm proud of you. But all of this trash talking you're doing tells me one thing: that you need an attitude adjustment, and when you get home, I'm just the one to give it to you!" Evidently she did, and evidently it worked, because that young man went on to become an all-American and then later a star in the National Basketball Association.

The point is clear. All of us from time to time need an attitude adjustment. We all need constantly to work on our attitudes, to take stock of where we've been and where we're going, how we can do better and how we can be better people.

Attitude adjustment: This is precisely what the apostle Paul was talking about in Philippians 3. In effect, he said, "I know that I'm not perfect, but I'm trying my best to be better because I have committed my life to Christ, and he deserves my best. So, forgetting what lies behind, forgetting my failures, forgetting my shortcomings, I strain forward to what lies ahead, and I press on toward the goal for the prize of the upward call of God in Christ Jesus" (vv. 12-14, paraphrased). Someone once put it like this: "I'm not all I could be. I'm not all I should be. I'm not all I'm going to be, but thank God, I'm not what I used to be."

Attitude is so crucial. So let me suggest some attitude adjustments we all need to make, some attitudes we all would do well to choose, some attitudes prescribed over and over again by the Bible and the Christian faith.

First of All, the Christian Faith Tells Us to Be Helpful, to Choose the Attitude of Helpfulness, to Commit Our Lives to That Spirit

If we asked the question, "What do you want most in life?" most people would answer, "To be happy." Well, the way to be happy is to be a helper!

Marian Preminger was born into enormous wealth. She was born in a castle in Hungary in 1913, to a rich aristocratic family. The castle had eighteen bedrooms and its own little chapel. It had a dining room with a table in it that would seat eighty-two people. Marian was reared in luxury: her grandmother, for example, insisted that they take their own linens on trips because she believed it beneath their dignity to sleep on sheets used by common people.

Marian attended school in Vienna when she was eighteen years old. She met and married a wealthy young man. That marriage lasted about a year. She stayed on in Vienna to pursue acting and met a young German director named Otto Preminger. After they were married, he got a contract to direct movies in Hollywood, where she began to live a rather scandalous life that was typical of Hollywood, especially in those days. Soon Otto Preminger divorced her.

Marian returned to Europe where she met Albert Schweitzer, who was in France on one of his periodic trips to raise funds for his missionary work in Africa. He was staying in a little village called Gunsbach. On a whim Marian called to see if she could get an appointment to see him. She was granted a visit the very next day. She went out to Gunsbach and found Schweitzer playing Bach on the organ in the village church. She sat and listened for a while until he noticed her.

Marian introduced herself. Albert Schweitzer asked, "Can you read music?" Marian said, "Yes." He asked her to be his page-turner as he played the organ, and later he asked her to stay for dinner. She joined his extended family, those people who always came to be with the great man. He presided over those meals like a German father, and he concluded them with scripture and the Lord's Prayer. At the end of the meal, Marian Preminger knew that her search for meaning was over. She went back to Africa with Albert Schweitzer, and she went to work in his hospital, serving and helping the poor.

This woman of privilege fed people suffering from leprosy who had no hands with which to feed themselves. And she felt happy and blessed and fulfilled. When Marian died, she was remembered as having said, "Albert Schweitzer said there are two classes of people in this world—the helpers, and the non-helpers. I'm a helper" (Maxie D. Dunnam, *The Communicator's Commentary: Galatians, Ephesians, Philippians, Colossians, Philemon* [Dallas: Word Books, 1979], 107-8).

On a higher level, we can all say that about Jesus Christ—"Because of him, I choose to be a helper." That's where Schweitzer got it in the first place, from Jesus. Jesus said, "If you will lose yourself in service to others, in love for others, in helpfulness to others, then you will find real life."

That's the first thing: The Christian faith tells us to be helpful, to choose the attitude of helpfulness.

Second, the Christian Faith Tells Us to Be Grateful, to Choose the Attitude of Appreciation

Whether we are age nine or ninety, it's the attitude of gratitude that keeps us young and vibrant and alive. And yet, it is easy to forget that. It is so easy to take life and its blessings for granted. If we are not tuned in to the attitude of appreciation, it is so easy to miss the joy of the present moment.

It is a sad commentary that some people go through life always wishing for more. And yet it is an apt description of many people, always wishing for something else, always seeing greener grass on the other side of the fence, and missing life because somehow they lost the attitude of appreciation.

A minister colleague of mine tells about asking his mother how her friend was doing. His mother said, "Why, son, she has been trying to die for years. Every time I see her or hear from her, she will say, 'I'm so glad to see you. But I probably won't see you tomorrow because things are mighty bad. I don't know that I will be here.'" And then the minister's mother added, "Son, if that woman ever worked as hard to live as she works to die, it's amazing to think how she might have enjoyed life!"

One of the best ways I know of to enjoy life is to live daily in the spirit of appreciation. On page after page, the Bible tells us to be helpful and to be grateful, to cultivate the attitude of helpfulness and the attitude of appreciation.

Third and Finally, the Christian Faith Tells Us to Be Trustful, to Choose the Attitude of Trust in God

We don't have to run scared. We don't have to be anxiety-ridden. We can trust in God. One of my favorite poems speaks to this. It listens in on two farmers in conversation. One asks the questions, and the other answers.

> Whatcha gonna do if the river overflow?
> Sit on the gallery and watch her go.
> Whatcha gonna do if your hogs all drown?
> Wish I'd lived on higher ground.
> Whatcha gonna do if your cow floats away?
> Throw in after her a bale of hay.
> Whatcha gonna do if your cabin leaves?
> Climb up on the roof and straddle the eaves.
> Whatcha gonna do when it comes on night?
> Trust in God and hold on tight!
> But whatcha gonna do if your strength gives way?
> Say "Howdy, Lord. It's Judgment Day!"

I like that old poem because it's about trusting God! It's about doing the best we can and then trusting God to bring it out right. It's about counting on God and believing that nothing, not even death, can separate us from God and God's love. We can trust God come what may, and God will always be there for us. That attitude of trust is a key to life. It gives us a confidence that is amazing. Someone once asked the great Christian Phillips Brooks why he was so serene and confident, and he said simply but profoundly, "Because I am a Christian, and I trust God!"

It is my prayer that God will give us an attitude adjustment, adjusting our attitudes to helpfulness, to appreciation, and, as never before, to trust in God.

13

How Is Love Best Expressed?

Mark 7:24-30

From there he set out and went away to the region of Tyre. He entered a house and did not want anyone to know he was there. Yet he could not escape notice, but a woman whose little daughter had an unclean spirit immediately heard about him, and she came and bowed down at his feet. Now the woman was a Gentile, of Syrophoenician origin. She begged him to cast the demon out of her daughter. He said to her, "Let the children be fed first, for it is not fair to take the children's food and throw it to the dogs." But she answered him, "Sir, even the dogs under the table eat the children's crumbs." Then he said to her, "For saying that, you may go—the demon has left your daughter." So she went home, found the child lying on the bed, and the demon gone.

I KNOW A HIGHLY RESPECTED INSPIRATIONAL SPEAKER, WHO, OVER THE last several years, has spent much of his time traveling around the world on speaking tours. Meanwhile, his wife has chosen to stay home and give herself and all that she has to the "bringing up" of their two children. On those rare occasions when she does travel with him, she finds herself engaged in conversations with some of the most accomplished, impressive, influential, sophisticated people in the world.

After one such trip, she told her husband that sometimes as she visits with these powerful people, she finds herself feeling intimidated and sometimes even questioning her own self-worth. He said to her, "Well, honey, why don't you come up with something you could say when you meet people that will let them know that you strongly value what you do and you feel that it is dramatically urgent and crucial and important?"

Well, not long after that, they were at a party, when a woman said to her, in a rather condescending tone, "Well, my dear, *what* do *you* do?" My friend heard his wife answer, "I am nurturing two *Homo sapiens* in the dominant values of the Judeo-Christian tradition, in order that they might become instruments for the transformation of the social order into the kind of eschatological utopia God envisioned from the beginning of time." And the other woman replied, "Oh, my; *I'm* just a *lawyer!*"

There are a lot of important jobs in the world today, but not one of them is more important than the job of being a mother. After all, who has a better opportunity to shape and influence and affect young lives than a mother? Let me share with you something that's been making the rounds recently. It's called "Somebody Said," and it has these words:

> Somebody said it takes about six weeks to get
> back to normal after you've had a baby ...
> *Somebody* doesn't know that once you're a
> mother, "normal" is history!
> Somebody said you learn how to be a mother by
> instinct ...
> *Somebody* never took a three-year-old shopping!
> Somebody said that being a mother is boring ...
> *Somebody* never rode in a car driven by a
> teenager with a driver's permit!
> Somebody said you don't need an education to
> be a mother ...
> *Somebody* never helped a fourth-grader with her
> math!
> Somebody said you can't love the fifth child as
> much as you love the first ...
> *Somebody* doesn't have five children!
> Somebody said the hardest part of being a

mother is labor and delivery ...
Somebody never watched her "baby" get on the
bus for the first day of kindergarten or on a
plane headed for military boot camp.
Somebody said your mother knows you love her,
so you don't need to tell her ...
Somebody isn't a mother.

Now, of course, the common thread that runs through all of these sayings is obvious: They are all about the love of a mother, and how that love can be expressed in words, attitudes, and actions.

That is precisely what we see in the Scripture in Mark 7, as this Greek mother comes to Jesus for help. Her daughter is sick, she has heard about Jesus and his power to heal. So as a loving, concerned mother, she comes to Jesus. She kneels before him and asks him to heal her daughter.

At first glance, it seems that Jesus is being a bit harsh with the woman because he says, "Let the children be fed first, for it is not fair to take the children's food and throw it to the dogs" (v. 27). What in the world does that mean? Well, the word *children* here refers to the Jews, and the word *dogs* refers to the Gentiles. The Jews regarded the Gentiles as ritually "unclean," and their most notorious term of contempt was to refer to the Gentiles as "dogs," the wild, filthy, flea-bitten dogs of the street. But, interestingly (don't miss this, now), Jesus does not use that word. In the original Greek text, he does not use that word, *dogs*. Rather, Jesus uses the diminutive word, which described not the filthy dogs of the street, but rather the little pet dogs of the house, the family's beloved puppies.

When he did that, the Greek woman realized immediately that Jesus was speaking with a smile, that she was with a friend, and that help was on the way. The woman was a Greek, and the Greeks of that day had a great love for conversation, dialogue, and friendly debate. They loved banter, repartee, mental sparring. Not only that, but back then, men did not discuss theological issues with women. Women back then were treated as inferior, as mindless, as things to be used, as chattel to be owned and discarded.

But look at this: Jesus honors her by including her in a philosophical, theological discussion, the kind that was so important in the Greek world of old. Because of this, the Greek woman understands that Jesus is befriending her, and she skillfully rises to the occasion with a brilliant response. She says, "Yes, I know the children are fed first, but surely I can have the crumbs under the table, which the children have thrown away" (v. 28, paraphrased).

Jesus loved this woman's response. He liked her spirit. Hers was a sunny faith that would not quit, a persistent faith that would not take "no" for an answer. Here was a mother with a sick child at home, who was willing to take a chance and go out on a limb for the sake of her child. When tested, she responded with grace and grit, with charm and insight. And Jesus was impressed. He liked her. He liked her boldness and her commitment to her child. And he answered her prayer. "You have answered well," he said to her. "And now you may go on your way, because your daughter has been made whole" (verse 29, paraphrased).

The Greek woman returned home quickly and found that indeed, her mission had been accomplished. Just as Jesus had said, her daughter was completely healed. The illness was totally gone. Jesus had, indeed, made her daughter well!

Now, this is a fascinating story, and at this point we could go in a number of different directions. We could look at the power of Jesus to heal, or the impact of the woman's bold persistence, or we could talk about how the Greek woman symbolizes all of the Gentiles and their inclusion in God's kingdom. But for now, let me invite you to look with me at the poignant portrait of love painted here. In this mother's encounter with Jesus, we see three of the most important ways to express love.

First of All, We Can Express Love with Words

Love can be expressed with words. The Greek woman came to Jesus that day to express in words her love for her sick child. Also, don't miss this: In the whole Gospel of Mark, she is the only person who lovingly calls Jesus "Lord."

It seems as though it would be so easy to express our love with words, but the truth is that precious few people do that well. Why is that? Why do we have trouble speaking the words of love? If we only realized how powerful words are, I think we would work harder at the task of expressing our love with words.

Some years ago, a woman was dying in a local hospital. She was in her mid-eighties. Her son flew in to be with her. I happened to be present when he arrived and entered the room. He walked over to the bedside of his dying mother. He leaned over and kissed her on the cheek. Then, touched by that tender moment of seeing her so weak and vulnerable and dying, he said to her, "Mom, you have been such a good mother to me. And I want you to know I love you." And through tears, the woman said, "Son, that's the first time you've ever told me. Last Friday was your sixty-third birthday, and that's the first time you ever told me." Isn't that something? It took him sixty-three years to say "I love you" to his mother.

Let me ask you something. Is there a word of love you need to speak today? Those of you fortunate enough to still have your parents—how long has it been since you told your mom or dad how much you love them and appreciate them? Or how long has it been since you told your mate? I don't mean a quick, routine, matter-of-fact "I love you," but a real heart-to-heart expression of your love in words.

And parents—how about you? How long has it been since you told your children how proud you are of them and how much you cherish them? Let me suggest something. For one week, write down every word you say to your children, and then ask yourself, how many of these words are words of love, encouragement, and appreciation, and not just words of correction or discipline? I know that as parents we have to be referees sometimes, and that is a loving thing to do. But also we need to be cheerleaders. We need to say, "I love you."

There is no question about it: one of the best ways to express love is with words.

Second, We Can Express Love with Attitude

We can express our love with our attitude toward life. One of the things about the Greek woman that impressed Jesus most was her attitude. She was committed to her child, and she was willing to do whatever it took to get help for her sick daughter. She was bold, determined, persistent, and courageous because she lived by the attitude of love. She would not be put off. She would not be discouraged. She would not give up, because she lived by the attitude of love.

Some years ago in a mining town in West Virginia, a seventeen-year-old boy took a summer job in the coal mines. Being a coal miner for the summer sounded adventuresome and macho.

However, the second week on the job, the young man got lost deep down in the mines. He had been working with a group of veteran miners. They had warned him. They had cautioned him. They had told him to stay close to the group because it would be so easy to get lost down there in the numerous caves and treacherous passageways of the mine. But he was seventeen years old, and one day, absentmindedly, he wandered away from his work-team, and he became lost, completely lost! He screamed for help, but the miners had moved on to another location, and no one could hear him.

Then, suddenly, his light went out, and he was in total darkness. He was absolutely terrified. He began to cry. He thought to himself: *This is how it all ends for me. I'm going to die down here. I don't know which way to go. I don't know how to get out.* The boy dropped down to his knees to pray. "O God, help me!" he said out loud. "O God, please help me!"

Then the young man noticed something. As he was kneeling there to pray, he felt his right knee touching something hard. He felt the object; it was a railroad track. He realized that if he kept his hand on that track and followed it, it would lead him out! That's what he did. He held on to the track and followed it, and eventually it brought him out of the dark, out of the depths of the mine, to light and safety.

That's a parable for us, isn't it? If we will hold on to the track of love and follow wherever it leads, if we will make love our attitude in life, no matter how dark some moments may be, the love-track will bring us out and lead us to the light. As clichéd as it may sound, it is still profoundly true: love is the answer, so we would do well to hold on to that track and to live by that attitude.

As Christians, that is our calling—to live always by the spirit and attitude of love. We can express our love with words and with attitude.

Third and Finally, We Can Express Love with Actions

That Greek mother in Mark 7 put her love to work. She acted it out. She expressed her love with actions. How important that is!

Some years ago, I went to college with a young woman from Southeast Asia. Her grandfather had been a headhunter. When she was in high school, she went one night to a youth program led by a Methodist college student. That night she was converted. She accepted Christ as her Savior and dedicated her life to him.

But then she had a problem: how would she tell her parents about her newfound faith? She decided to not tell them in words, but rather to show them in deeds of love. Here's how she described what happened. She said, "Before Christ came into my life, I was spoiled and selfish. I was irritable and impatient. I was disrespectful to my parents. My room was a mess, and my attitude was worse. But after Christ came into my life, I changed. I was kind to my parents. I cleaned up my room. I helped with the housework. I spoke to my parents with tenderness and respect. I was loving toward everyone. My parents noticed, and they said to me, 'You are different! Why? What has happened to you?'"

She said to them, "Yes, I am different because I have been reborn! I have Christ as my Savior. I am a Christian now, and Christians always live by the law of love."

And her parents said, "Tell us more of this religion. Tell us more of this Christ. If he can change people like that, we want to be Christians too!"

Well, that's the way it works. We can express our love with words and with attitude, but most powerfully, most dramatically, and most meaningfully, with actions!

14

What Is the Essential Spirit of the Christian?

Philippians 4:4-7 (NEB)

Farewell; I wish you all joy in the Lord. I will say it again: all joy be yours.

Let your magnanimity be manifest to all.

The Lord is near; have no anxiety, but in everything make your requests known to God in prayer and petition with thanksgiving. Then the peace of God, which is beyond our utmost understanding, will keep guard over your hearts and your thoughts, in Christ Jesus.

SOMEONE ONCE SAID, "YOU CAN CALL ME ANYTHING, IF YOU WILL LET me define the terms." So I want us to define the term *magnanimity*, because it was such an important word to the apostle Paul and such a key characteristic in the life of Jesus.

Writing a long time ago to the Philippian Christians, Paul called the spirit of magnanimity the essential spirit of the Christian. He told the Philippians that a Christian should be characterized by his or her magnanimity, and that the spirit of magnanimity should be dramatically obvious to others—not silent and secretive, but radiant and infectious, as bright as the sunlight. Here's how Paul put it: "Let your magnanimity be manifest to all" (Philippians 4:5, NEB).

But, what is *magnanimity*? Well, it's a million-dollar word for a much, much richer spirit. The dictionary defines *magnanimity* as "the quality of being big in spirit, gentle, kind, considerate, thoughtful, respectful, rising above pettiness or meanness, forgiving, gracious, generous in overlooking injury or insult." *Roget's Thesaurus* links magnanimity with greatness, nobility, high-mindedness, big-heartedness; it's the opposite of pettiness or littleness. Magnanimity could well be called the noblest of human graces. Let me paint its picture for us.

For example, we see the spirit of magnanimity dramatically in Abraham Lincoln. Lincoln was a big man, a man big in spirit. He showed amazing magnanimity, especially toward General McClellan, whom he appointed (for a time) to command the armies of the North in the War Between the States. McClellan was a brash young upstart, an obnoxious, arrogant man who treated President Lincoln terribly. Yet because Lincoln respected and trusted McClellan as a soldier, he suffered his personal insults with grace and patience.

One evening, President Lincoln and a colleague went to General McClellan's home on a matter of urgency concerning the war. Of course, people normally go to the President, but Lincoln, trying to be friendly and wanting not to inconvenience McClellan, came to his home.

After keeping the President waiting for a long time, McClellan finally sent word down by a servant that he was just too tired to see President Lincoln. Lincoln's colleague was indignant. Other cabinet members, upon hearing about this, wanted McClellan kicked out immediately for this insubordination and rudeness. But Lincoln only smiled and replied, "I will gladly hold General McClellan's stirrup for him, if he will only win us victories!" That's magnanimity!

Earlier, Edwin Stanton had publicly denounced Abraham Lincoln as a "fool," "a low, cunning clown." Stanton called Lincoln "the original gorilla," venomous, hateful words. But do you know what President Lincoln did? He appointed Stanton as the Secretary of War because he truly believed that Stanton was the best man for the job. That's magnanimity!

We also see it in that famous poem written by Edwin Markham. Markham had been hurt and betrayed by a trusted friend, but he worked through the pain and wrote these classic words:

> He drew a circle that shut me out.
> Heretic, rebel, a thing to flout,

But Love and I had the wit to win:
We drew a circle that took him in.
("Outwitted," ca. 1899)

That's magnanimity!
We see it also in Dr. Booker T. Washington, the great African American educator. The story goes that one day as Professor Washington was walking to work at the famous Tuskegee Institute in Alabama, he happened to pass the mansion of a very wealthy woman. The woman didn't recognize Booker T. Washington, and she called out to him, thinking he was one of her workers: "Hey, you, come here. I need some wood chopped!" Without a word, Professor Washington peeled off his jacket, picked up the ax, and went to work. He not only cut a large pile of wood, but he also carried the firewood into the house and arranged it neatly by the fireplace.

He had scarcely left when a house servant said to the woman, "I guess you didn't recognize him, ma'am, but that was Professor Washington!" Embarrassed and red-faced, the woman hurried over to Tuskegee Institute to apologize. Booker T. Washington said to her, "There's no need to apologize, Madam. I am delighted to do favors for my friends!" That's magnanimity! By the way, that woman (from that moment on) became one of Tuskegee Institute's warmest and most generous supporters.

This story just underscores how magnanimous Booker T. Washington was day-in and day-out. He absolutely refused to be disturbed by insults or rudeness or persecution. He once said, "I will permit no man to narrow and degrade my soul by making me hate him." That's magnanimity!

But, of course, we see the best portrait of magnanimity in Jesus Christ. He taught it in the Sermon on the Mount:

"Go the second mile."
"Turn the other cheek."
"Give your cloak as well as your coat."
"Love your enemies."
"Pray for those who persecute you."
"Be merciful like your Father in heaven is merciful." (see Matthew 5–7)

That's magnanimity!

But Jesus didn't just teach it, didn't just talk about it; he *lived* magnanimously! Think of it, Jesus saying, "Let the children come to me," and then taking them up in his arms.

Jesus saying tenderly to the woman taken in adultery, "Neither do I condemn you; go and sin no more."

Jesus on the cross, praying, "Father, forgive them, they know not what they do."

That's magnanimity—a good word for our vocabularies, and a great spirit for our lives.

The Gospels make it clear that Jesus made the spirit of magnanimity the primary aim of those who live the Christian lifestyle and the key test of Christian character. In essence, he put it like this: "If you will live with a big heart and a big spirit, and if you will love unconditionally like I do, then people will know that you are my disciples" (John 13:34-35, paraphrased). But the question is, how are we doing with this? Is our magnanimity obvious to everybody? Can people see and feel this Christlike spirit in us?

To bring this closer to home, let me list three special qualities of the magnanimous person.

First of All, the Magnanimous Person Is Big Enough to Look for the Best in Other People

That is, the magnanimous person is slow to condemn others and quick to praise them. The magnanimous person speaks graciously and kindly and avoids gossip and destructive criticism.

In his book *This Is Living*, Leonard Griffith says it well:

> Criticism, the favorite indoor sport of small minds, is odious to a Christian. When its ugly stench fills the air around him, and people begin babbling pontifically about the faults of other people, the Christian feels inclined to open a window and shut his own mouth. He witnesses by his silence. But, that is not enough, writes Paul. Silence can too easily be taken to mean assent. If you believe in judging people generously, if you believe in withholding any judgment until you have learned the facts, if you think that people in glass houses ought not to throw stones, if you have too much respect for human personality to damage it with your tongue or

pen, if you believe that the Christian thing to do is to always give [others] the benefit of the doubt—then, *say so* and say it so that everyone can hear. (Leonard Griffith, *This Is Living* [Nashville/New York: Abingdon Press, 1966], 122)

Let your magnanimity be manifest to all! As Christians, we are called to speak good, not evil; kindness, not cruelty; love, not hate. Recently, I was in a college town on a speaking engagement. One evening I went into a diner near my hotel to get a bite to eat. In the large booth next to me was a group of college students. I didn't mean to eavesdrop, but they were talking loudly and dramatically and critically. They were gossiping about one of their classmates, a sophomore girl named Cathy. Maybe "gossiping" is not a strong enough word; they were *lambasting* Cathy, criticizing her harshly, crucifying her with hard, cruel words. All of them were having a field day ripping her apart with tough, condemning words. All of them, that is, except one young man, whose name was George. George just sat there in silence, not participating at all in the harsh roasting of their classmate.

Finally, the others realized that George was not saying anything, so they tried to pull him into the verbal onslaught. "George, what do you think? Isn't it awful how Cathy has been acting? They ought to kick her out of school. We wish they would! She is a disgrace to our class, the way she just throws herself at every guy who comes along. She is an embarrassment! Don't you agree, George?"

I love what George did. He sat there quietly for a moment, and then he said, "You know, I have way too many faults of my own to be critical of Cathy, or, for that matter, to be critical of anybody. Besides that, I *like* Cathy. She is my friend. She is *our* friend, and she has so many wonderful qualities. I think we should focus on those good things. She is really a lot of fun, and I hope that someday you all can get to know her better and appreciate her more, like I do. Besides that, my mom taught me an important lesson some years ago that I have tried my best to live by daily. She said, 'George, remember this: brilliant people talk about ideas; ordinary people talk about things; little people talk about other people.'"

Let me ask you something. Can you go a week without saying

something critical about another person? Can you go a day without gossiping? Can you go twenty-four hours without being judgmental toward others? Can you go twelve hours? Or eight? If you can't, then you have a big problem.

If a person can't go a day without alcohol, then we say that person is an alcoholic and needs help. That person is addicted to alcohol.

If a person can't go a day without abusing drugs, then we say that person is a drug addict and has a huge problem and desperately needs help.

If a person can't go a day without gambling, then we say we need to get that person to a gambling recovery group immediately, because that person has a gambling problem that can ruin his or her life.

The same is true with gossiping or being judgmental or being harshly critical. If you can't go a day without condemning other people, then you have a problem because you are addicted to that kind of negative hurtful behavior.

Magnanimity is the opposite of that. Magnanimity is big enough to always look for the best in other people. Magnanimity is wrapped in grace because it realizes (as George put it) that we all have way too many faults of our own to be critical of anybody else. We all have our big share of sins and weaknesses and failures and frailties. We all have "clay feet," so much so, that our only hope is in the amazing grace of God. God is so kind and gracious and patient with us. How could we not be kind and gracious toward others!

That's number one: Magnanimous people are big enough to look for the best in other people.

Second, Magnanimous People Are Big Enough to Be Loving Toward Others

His name is Jim. He is a member of our church and a good friend of mine. He and his wife live in a beautiful home in Sugar Land, and they are members of one of the finest country clubs in the area. The Saturday morning after Hurricane Katrina hit the Gulf Coast and 26,000 evacuees were brought to the Astrodome in Houston, Jim got up early, put on his casual clothes and headed out to meet with the members of his investment group, who were holding their meeting on the campus of the University of Houston that morning.

On the way to the meeting, Jim stopped at a fast-food restaurant beside the Astrodome for breakfast. When he got to the counter, he ordered a breakfast taco and a cup of coffee for four dollars and eleven cents.

Now, Jim has a habit of doing what many men do. Each night, he puts his spare change in a bowl, and every now and then he gathers up all of those pennies, nickels, dimes, and quarters and takes them to a bank or a store or a restaurant, and he spends the change so that he doesn't have to carry all of those coins around in his pocket every day. Jim had decided to do just that on that Saturday morning at the restaurant. So while the staff were preparing his breakfast taco and coffee, Jim began to place on the counter all of his spare change, pennies, nickels, dimes, and quarters, in neat stacks, carefully counting it to be sure that he had exactly $4.11 laid out on the restaurant counter.

But when they brought his breakfast to the counter, a surprising thing happened. The young couple in line behind Jim, who had been watching him meticulously count out his small change, stepped forward and said, "We would like to buy this gentleman's breakfast!" Jim was stunned by their offer, and he protested, but they insisted. They would not take no for an answer, and they bought his breakfast at the fast-food restaurant beside the Astrodome because they thought he was one of the Katrina survivors. Jim even pulled out his billfold to show them that he had money, but the young couple probably thought it was the two thousand dollars the survivors in the Astrodome had been given by FEMA the day before!

The next day at church, Jim told this story to his Sunday school class. He said that he was so moved and touched by the thoughtfulness and generosity and kindness of that young couple that he, in turn, wanted to pay it forward. He wanted to give ten times the price of his Saturday-morning breakfast to a special fund his Sunday school class had that supported the Christian Community Service Center, one of the great agencies in our city that helps needy people.

Let me hurry to tell you that I don't know anything about that generous couple who bought Jim's breakfast that Saturday morning, but my guess would be that they learned to do "random acts of kindness" like that from their faith. They learned it at church and at Sunday school. My guess would be that they learned to do beautiful things like that from Jesus because that is what he taught. Don't wait around to be asked. Just do it! Reach out to people with love and grace, with acts of compassion and goodwill and generosity. "Love others," Jesus said, "as I have loved you." That's magnanimity, the spirit of big-heartedness that enables the people who have it to be sensitive and thoughtful and gracious as they reach out in love to family, to friends, to colleagues, to neighbors, and, yes, even to strangers!

In the aftermath of Hurricane Katrina, who were the people all over the country who immediately rolled up their sleeves and rushed to welcome the survivors, to help them, to hug them, to encourage them, and to support them with their service and donations? I'll tell you who it was, it was the church people, the people of faith, hope, and love, the people of magnanimity, who first always look for the best in others, and who second are sensitive and thoughtful and loving toward others.

Third and Finally, Magnanimous People Are Big Enough to Forgive and Forget

Magnanimous people don't hold grudges. They don't seek vengeance.

Some years ago, a woman in New England was going through a grief experience, and she became bitter and angry, and for some reason she took it all out on her minister. She said horrible things about him, started terrible rumors about him, wrote cruel letters to him, and made calls, trying everything to get him fired. And through it all, the minister kept on being kind to her.

Later she moved to another section of the country, joined a new church, and got involved in a wonderful Sunday school class. As she studied the Scriptures and as she worked through her grief, she was drawn closer to Christ, and then she realized how horribly she had treated her former minister. She was so ashamed and penitent. She sat down and wrote him a letter apologizing for the harsh way she had treated him and asking him if he could find it in his heart to forgive her. She wrote, "After all I have done to you and all the pain I have caused you, I wouldn't blame you if you can't forgive me, but I hope and pray that you will."

A few days later, she received a letter from that minister. It had three words: "Forgiven...Forgotten...Forever!"

Can you do that? Can you forgive like that? That's magnanimity: it's being big enough to always look for the best in others, to be thoughtful and loving toward others, and to be able to forgive and forget.

15

How Does Faith Help Us Face the Storms of Life?

Matthew 14:22-33

Immediately he made the disciples get into the boat and go on ahead to the other side, while he dismissed the crowds. And after he had dismissed the crowds, he went up the mountain by himself to pray. When evening came, he was there alone, but by this time the boat, battered by the waves, was far from the land, for the wind was against them. And early in the morning he came walking toward them on the sea. But when the disciples saw him walking on the sea, they were terrified, saying, "It is a ghost!" And they cried out in fear. But immediately Jesus spoke to them and said, "Take heart, it is I; do not be afraid."

Peter answered him, "Lord, if it is you, command me to come to you on the water." He said, "Come." So Peter got out of the boat, started walking on the water, and came toward Jesus. But when he noticed the strong wind, he became frightened, and beginning to sink, he cried out, "Lord, save me!" Jesus immediately reached out his hand and caught him, saying to him, "You of little faith, why did you doubt?" When they got into the boat, the wind ceased. And those in the boat worshiped him, saying, "Truly you are the Son of God."

FAITH IS THE ANSWER, BUT WHAT ARE THE QUESTIONS?

A MAN ONCE CAME TO A FARMER AND ASKED TO BE TAKEN ON AS A hired hand. "What can you do?" the farmer asked him. The man replied, "I can sleep when the wind blows." The farmer thought that was a strange answer; but he needed a worker, so he hired him.

Soon after, the farmer went away on a trip. A couple of weeks later, the farmer returned home one night and went to bed. But a storm came up. Winds were blowing and lashing. The farmer awoke and heard the winds, and he remembered the broken barn door, the weak place in the fence, and some ripped wire in the chicken coop.

Concerned about his livestock, the farmer got up and went out into the storm to check on them, and what do you think he found? The barn door, the fence, and the chicken coop all had been repaired. The animals were all safe, and the hired worker was sleeping soundly. Then the farmer remembered what the man had said: "I can sleep when the wind blows." He could sleep because he had prepared ahead for the storm! As we learned dramatically from Hurricanes Katrina and Rita, it is so important, so crucial, to prepare ahead for the storm, so vital to have the resources we need when we are caught in a storm.

There is a powerful story about this in the Gospel of Matthew. The disciples of Jesus (not having Doppler radar or twenty-four-hour weather coverage) get caught in a frightening storm out in the middle of the Sea of Galilee. As the disciples are rowing against the wind, scared, tired, frustrated, drained, depleted, Christ comes to them in an incredible way, walking on the water!

Isn't it fascinating that the presence of Christ is often most visible and most welcome when we are caught in a storm and rowing against the wind? Remember this amazing story with me. It's a miracle-story, but it is also a parable-story. It's like a parable acted out. It deals with the frustration and helplessness we sometimes feel. It deals with the hard struggles of life. It deals with the overwhelming flood of problems that rush in against us and pour down upon us. But it also reminds us that in the difficult moments, in the storms of life, in those flood-tide moments when we feel that we are about to be overcome and swept under, Christ comes to us in powerful and dramatic ways, bringing help and strength, peace and poise, confidence and victory.

Remember the context of the story. Jesus has just finished feeding the multitude with the five loaves and two fish. He has sent the crowd away, their bodies satisfied. Now, he must feed himself, not with food for the body, but for his spirit. Jesus sends the disciples ahead by boat to their next destination, while he goes up on a mountain to pray. In prayer and meditation, in thought and quiet time alone, Jesus will again commune with his heavenly Father to recharge his spiritual life and renew the spiritual strength of his soul in preparation for the new challenges that he will soon face.

Now, the disciples are out on the Sea of Galilee without him. The New Testament seems determined to call this famous body of water a "sea." Again and again, the writers call it "the Sea of Galilee." Actually, it's more like a lake. It's only about seven miles wide and only some thirteen miles long; but regardless of its small size, it could "kick up" a large-sized storm and could indeed be quite treacherous.

Winds could quite quickly come up from nowhere around those hills and stir up the waves into a fury of rage and storm. In such a storm, the lake took on the threat of a big sea, and people on the water needed to be very, very careful. Crossing the lake could be a simple venture if the wind were with you and if your sails were turned to catch it; but if there were no wind, then you would have to row! You would have to put your muscle into it. Even then, the task, though not as pleasant as sailing, would have been manageable enough.

However, on this occasion in Matthew's Gospel, the disciples find themselves facing a number of difficult obstacles. First of all, it is nighttime, and consequently, visibility is a real problem for them. They're out there in the dark.

Not only that but also it is cloudy because of the storm that is brewing, and they can't see the stars or follow them, so they are having trouble getting their sense of direction.

Add to that the fact that the wind of the storm is not *with* them, but *against* them, so their sails are useless.

On top of all of that, not only do they have to row the boat, but they are rowing against the wind—into the face of the storm. They are not getting anywhere. The writer puts it like this: They are being "battered by the waves" (Matthew 14:24).

There they are, out there in the storm, being tossed to and fro, making no progress—tired, frustrated, drained, depleted, scared to death, confused, and probably a little miffed at Jesus for sending them out there.

"Where is the Master now?"

"Where is he now when we need him so desperately?"

"We are tired, worn, defeated."

"We are in danger of being overwhelmed and drowned in the deep!"

Can you identify with the disciples' plight? Can you relate? Don't we all have moments like that, when we feel stormed over and worn out? The storms and pressures and troubles of this world lash against us, and our Lord doesn't seem to be around.

But then, look what happens. The Lord sees their dilemma. He is aware of their plight, and he goes straight toward them. He has been close by all along, closer even than they realized, and he comes to them. He comes to help them. He comes to save them. Through the wind, the storm, the danger, the chaos, the disorder, the disruption, he comes to them!

That's the way Jesus comes to us, isn't it? He comes sometimes when we least expect him and most need him. He comes in the dead of the night, in the thick of the storm. When it's darkest and most tumultuous, that's when he comes most vividly.

Now, look at the remarkable courage of Simon Peter here: "Lord, if it's you," he says, "let me come to you on the water" (v. 28, paraphrased). Christ says, "Come," and Peter, too, walks on the water for a moment, but then his eyes go back to the winds and the waves, and fear takes over, and he begins to sink.

His Lord reaches over and pulls him out. And as they get into the boat, the storm subsides, the winds stop, and there is calm. And there is a sermon there somewhere!

William Barclay has a fascinating comment about this story. Here are his words:

> See what happened. Immediately, [when] Jesus saw His friends in trouble His own problems were set aside; the moment for prayer was past; the time for action had come; He forgot himself and went

to the help of His friends. That is the very essence of Jesus. The cry of human need to Him surpassed all other claims. His friends needed Him; He must go.

[All of] what happened we do not know, and will never know. The story is cloaked in mystery which defies explanation. What we do know is that He came to them and their storm became a calm. With Him beside them nothing mattered any more....

It is the simple fact of life, a fact which has been proved by countless thousands of men and women in every generation, that when Christ is there the storm becomes a calm, the tumult becomes a peace, the undoable becomes doable, the unbearable becomes bearable, and [people] pass the breaking point and do not break. To walk with Christ will be for us also the conquest of the storm. (William Barclay, *The Gospel of Mark*, 2nd ed., The Daily Study Bible [Philadelphia: Westminster Press, 1956], 163)

Now, with all of this as a backdrop for our thinking, let me underscore three important lessons for us that flow out of this dramatic story in Matthew 14. Here's number one.

First of All, We All Get Caught in the Storms of Life

It is a fact that life has its storms. Life is not an easy ride across a smooth, flat plateau. It gets bumpy sometimes. We all know that too well. There are mountaintops and valleys. Things don't always go just as we want them to go.

Sometimes the winds blow against us.

Sometimes we feel overwhelmed by the flood-tides of life.

Sometimes we feel burdened and crushed and weighted down.

Sometimes we have to "row against the wind."

Recently, a man came into the office area of our church looking for help. He was deeply troubled. You could tell it by looking at him. He looked worn and weary, his face was drawn, his eyes were tired, his expression was sad, and his shoulders were slumped over as if he were carrying a heavy load. Then, almost as if on cue, he said it: "I'm scared, worried, exhausted, depleted. I feel like I'm carrying hundred pound weights on my back all the time. I am a burdened man." When he said that, he expressed what many people are feeling these days. Tremendously difficult problems "weigh down" upon us and threaten to crush the life out of us.

Think of it: inflation, depression, pollution, crime, fear, anxiety, grief, heartache, pressure, stress. We had just as well admit it: life, for many people today, has become a strained and somber business. They feel heavy-laden, cast down, burdened. They feel as though they are caught in a storm and rowing against the wind.

Now, here is a place, the Scriptures tell us, where faith can help. We can cast our burdens on the Lord, and he shall sustain us. If we will keep rowing and look to him with the eyes of faith, he will come to our aid, he will come with strength and peace and confidence.

This brings us to lesson number two.

Second, When We Are in These Difficult, Stormy Situations, Christ Comes to Us in Special Ways

If I were to ask you to recall those moments in your life when you felt God's presence most vividly, most dramatically, most powerfully, there might be a few who would recall a worship experience, or a few who would remember a joyous event or a victorious moment, but most of us would remember how God came to us in a stormy situation—a time of sorrow or sadness, a time of tragedy or crisis, a time of sickness or injury, a time of misfortune or heartache.

Some years ago, some good friends of ours suddenly and tragically lost their youngest daughter. Her name was Ellen. She was sitting in the den at home one evening, laughing and talking with her mother.

With no warning, Ellen's leg went numb, and then her arms. Then she fell back, paralyzed, and quickly she fell into a deep coma. She was rushed to the hospital, where all-night brain surgery was performed. Ellen died the next day, just sixteen years old.

When I called to express my love and sympathy, Ellen's parents said, "God is giving us strength we didn't know we could have. He is holding us up and seeing us through this. We got to have Ellen for sixteen years, and she packed more life and love into sixteen years than most people do in a lifetime. We are crushed, but we are all right. Don't worry about us because God is with us. We can feel his presence nearer than breathing. We can feel his presence as never before."

When we are caught in the storm, God comes in special ways to bring strength and help and hope.

Now, here is lesson number three.

Third and Finally, in These Kinds of Situations, When Our Eyes Are Fixed on Christ, We Can Do Incredible Things; and When We Take Our Eyes Off of Him, We Sink

Simon Peter looked at Christ, and he walked on water. When he took his eyes off of Christ and looked at the waves, he got scared, and he began to sink.

Some years ago, a little girl was very excited because her father was going to take her to see the movie *Snow White.* Someone asked the little girl, "But won't you be scared of the wicked witch?"

"No," the little girl said. "When the witch comes on, I won't look at her. I'll just look at my father!"

That's the way it works, isn't it? When we fix our eyes on Christ, we can do incredible things. This is the good news of the gospel and the bottom line of its message. Even when facing life's storms, we need not be afraid if we look to Christ.

Suggestions for Leading a Study of *Faith Is the Answer, but What Are the Questions?*

John D. Schroeder

This book by James W. Moore emphasizes that when it comes to faith, it's important not only that we find the right answers but also that we ask the right questions. To assist you in facilitating a discussion group, this study guide was created to help make this experience beneficial for both you and members of your group. Here are some thoughts on how you can help your group:

1. Distribute the book to participants before your first meeting and request that they come having read the first chapter. You may want to limit the size of your group to increase participation.
2. Begin your sessions on time. Your participants will appreciate your promptness. You may wish to begin your first session with introductions and a brief get-acquainted time. Start each session by reading aloud the snapshot summary of the chapter for the day.
3. Select discussion questions and activities in advance. Note that the first question is a general question designed to get discussion going. The last question is designed to summarize the discussion. Feel free to change the order of the listed questions and to create your own questions. Allow a set amount of time for the questions and activities.
4. Remind participants that all questions are valid as part of the learning process. Encourage their participation in discussion by saying there are no "wrong" answers and that all input will be

appreciated. Invite participants to share their thoughts, personal stories, and ideas as their comfort level allows.

5. Some questions may be more difficult to answer than others. If you ask a question and no one responds, begin the discussion by venturing an answer yourself. Then ask for comments and other answers. Remember that some questions may have multiple answers.

6. Ask the question "Why?" or "Why do you believe that?" to help continue a discussion and give it greater depth.

7. Give everyone a chance to talk. Keep the conversation moving. Occasionally you may want to direct a question to a specific person who has been quiet. "Do you have anything to add?" is a good follow-up question to ask another person. If the topic of conversation gets off track, move ahead by asking the next question in your study guide.

8. Before moving from questions to activities, ask group members if they have any questions that have not been answered. Remember that as a leader, you do not have to know all the answers. Some answers may come from group members. Other answers may even need a bit of research. Your job is to keep the discussion moving and to encourage participation.

9. Review the activity in advance. Feel free to modify it or to create your own activity. Encourage participants to try the "At home" activity.

10. Following the conclusion of the activity, close with a brief prayer, praying either the printed prayer from the study guide or a prayer of your own. If your group desires, pause for individual prayer petitions.

11. Be grateful and supportive. Thank group members for their ideas and participation.

12. You are not expected to be a "perfect" leader. Just do the best you can by focusing on the participants and the lesson. God will help you lead this group.

13. Enjoy your time together!

Suggestions for Participants

1. What you will receive from this study will be in direct proportion to your involvement. Be an active participant!

2. Please make it a point to attend all sessions and to arrive on time so that you can receive the greatest benefit.

3. Read the chapter and review the study guide questions prior to the meeting. You may want to jot down questions you have from the reading and also answers to some of the study guide questions.

4. Be supportive and appreciative of your group leader as well as the other members of your group. You are on a journey together.

5. Your participation is encouraged. Feel free to share your thoughts about the material being discussed.

6. Pray for your group and your leader.

Introduction:
Faith Is the Answer, but What Are the Questions?

Snapshot Summary
This chapter looks at what it means to be a Christian and how Jesus is our example to follow in committing to God, loving others, and celebrating life.

Reflection / Discussion Questions
1. Share a time when you waited for or sought an important answer.

2. Reflect on / discuss the importance of asking questions, especially questions of faith.

3. Describe how it feels to be lost or uncertain what to do next.

4. What was the problem of the rich young ruler? What did he have, and what did he lack?

5. What does Jesus teach us about commitment to God?

6. What lessons do we learn from Jesus about loving others?

7. In what ways can we show our love for God?

8. Reflect on / discuss what provides true joy in life.

9. Why do we need to celebrate life? How is this done?

10. Reflect / discuss: What are some of the key questions of faith you would like to explore in more depth?

Activities

As a group: Using your Bibles, locate and discuss important questions of faith asked by biblical characters.

At home: Give yourself permission this week to ask questions and seek answers to issues important to you and your family.

Prayer: *Dear God, thank you for providing faith to help us find our way. Help us ask the right questions, that we may find the answers we need to live a life of service and love, in the example of your Son, Jesus Christ. Amen.*

Chapter 1
To Whom Will We Give Our Allegiance?
In Whom Will We Put Our Trust?

Snapshot Summary

This chapter reminds us to remember God in times of uncertainty, when shortcuts tempt us, and when we face death.

Reflection / Discussion Questions

1. Reflect on / discuss why people often lose sight of the difference between what is important and what is not.
2. Share your system of reminding yourself of important dates or events.
3. In Deuteronomy 6, what reminder did Moses give the people, and why?
4. In what way is the Great Commandment as relevant today as it was in the time of Moses?
5. As you are comfortable doing so, share a difficult time in your life when you faced an uncertain future.
6. How have the promises of God helped you through life?
7. Describe some shortcuts people are tempted to take.
8. Reflect on / discuss strategies to resist shortcuts and other temptations. What works for you?
9. What do we need to remember about God when it comes to facing death?

10. What can we learn about allegiance and trust from reading this chapter?

Activities
As a group: Let each person share something he or she would like to remember from this chapter. Use art supplies to create a bookmark containing the messages you want to remember.

At home: This week, tie a string around your finger or use some other memory device to remember the importance of placing your trust in God.

Prayer: *Dear God, thank you for being there for us in times of trouble and uncertainty. Help us remember to put our trust in you. Amen.*

Chapter 2
Why Believe in Jesus?

Snapshot Summary
This chapter reminds us of the gifts that Jesus gives us, including a self you can live with, a faith to live by, and a love you can live out.

Reflection / Discussion Questions
1. Share the origins of your spiritual faith. Who helped make you a believer?
2. Why were the early followers of Jesus so committed to him?
3. What do you admire about Paul and Silas, as described in Acts 16:25-34?
4. How and why was the jailer changed through the faith of Paul and Silas?
5. Explain the importance of having a self you can live with.
6. What lessons can we learn from what happened to Paul on the road to Damascus?
7. In your own words, explain what it means to have a faith you can live by.
8. Give an example of how Christians can serve as conduits of Christ's love.

9. How would you answer the question posed in the title of this chapter, "Why believe in Jesus?"
10. How does God's love change your life?

Activities
As a group: Jesus is our guide, our teacher, and our measuring stick. Create a measuring stick with units of measurement indicating values and qualities that Jesus has and wants us to possess.

At home: Reflect upon why you believe in Jesus. Consider how your faith is reflected in your words and actions.

Prayer: *Dear God, thank you for being our faithful leader. Help us look to you for answers in life and know that you walk with us every day. Amen.*

Chapter 3
What Does It Mean to Build Your Life on Jesus Christ?

Snapshot Summary
   This chapter reminds us to stay connected to Christ's servant mentality, to Christ's great promise, and to Christ's amazing grace.

Reflection / Discussion Questions
1. Reread John 15:1-5. In your own words, what is Jesus saying in this scripture passage?
2. What mistakes do people make when trying to put their lives together?
3. How is the Bible similar to an instruction manual?
4. Explain what it means to be a Christian servant. What are your duties as a Christian?
5. Reflect on / discuss ways to stay connected to Christ's servant mentality.
6. Reflect on / discuss the benefits that Christ's great promise provides believers today.
7. Share a time when you relied upon Christ's great promise.
8. What is meant by the phrase "Our only hope is the grace of God"?

9. What additional thoughts or ideas from this chapter would you like to explore?
10. How can we help others *get* or *stay* connected to Christ?

Activities

As a group: List and then share what you would pack into an assembly kit for building a strong Christian faith.

At home: Reflect upon how you are connected to God and to others. How do these connections help you? What obligations do they require?

Prayer: *Dear God, thank you for providing the right connections to live a healthy Christian life. Help us build our lives upon Christ and be of service to others. Amen.*

Chapter 4
When Do We Feel God's Pleasure?

Snapshot Summary

This chapter shows how we feel God's pleasure when we forgive others, when we include others, and when we love the way Christ loved.

Reflection / Discussion Questions
1. Share a time when you felt God's pleasure.
2. What did the prophet Micah say about pleasing God?
3. How is what gives humans pleasure different from what gives God pleasure?
4. Explain what it means to take on the spirit of Jesus Christ.
5. How did Pope John Paul II demonstrate forgiveness?
6. What does it mean to forgive the way Christ forgave?
7. Define *inclusive*, and give an example of it.
8. In what ways did Jesus demonstrate inclusive love?
9. How was Jesus' teaching of love different from the typical customs and practices in his day?
10. What are some other ways we can please God that are not mentioned in this chapter?

Activities

As a group: Jesus called us to build bridges. Create a group list of ways we can construct bridges of love, forgiveness, and inclusiveness.

At home: Reflect upon how you personally bring pleasure to God. Examine your words and actions during this week as you seek to model your life after Christ's.

Prayer: *Dear God, thank you for reminding us of the ways we can please you and serve others. Help us build bridges at home, at work, and at church, and throughout our lives. Amen.*

Chapter 5
Why Can Christians Face Death Triumphantly?
O Death, Where Is Thy Victory?
O Grave, Where Is Thy Sting?

Snapshot Summary

This chapter shows us how Easter makes it possible for us to be people of hope, people of love, and people of victory.

Reflection / Discussion Questions
1. In your own words, what does it mean to face death triumphantly?
2. Name some reminders Easter gives us each year.
3. Name some reasons why people fear death and dying.
4. As you have grown older, what have you learned about death?
5. As the author tells us, "The risen Lord called Mary by name"; what does this mean for us today?
6. Reflect on / discuss the connection between Easter and hope that is alive.
7. How do people of hope behave and talk?
8. What lessons do we learn from Easter about the power of love?
9. Reflect on / discuss what it means to be people of victory. How do people of victory live?
10. What additional thoughts or ideas from this chapter would you like to explore?

Activities
As a group: Make a list of symbols of Easter, and talk about what each symbol represents.

At home: Reflect upon life and death. Pray, thanking God for victory over death in the risen Christ.

Prayer: *Dear God, thank you for giving us victory over death and the grave. Help us celebrate life and live a life that is pleasing to you. Amen.*

Chapter 6
What Are the Dramatic Signs of a Healthy Faith?

Snapshot Summary
This chapter reminds us of the importance of having a healthy relationship with God, with others, and with yourself.

Reflection / Discussion Questions
1. Reflect on / discuss the importance of having a healthy sense of humor.
2. What are some of the things that contribute to a person's physical health?
3. What are some of the things that make a person unhealthy, both spiritually and physically?
4. How can you tell if your relationship with God is healthy or unhealthy?
5. What are some of the benefits of having a healthy relationship with God?
6. What are some of the things we can do to maintain a healthy relationship with God?
7. What can we learn from the relationship Jesus had with his Father?
8. According to the author, what is the promise of Pentecost?
9. Why is it important to have a healthy relationship with others?
10. What are some of the keys to having a healthy relationship with yourself?

Activities

As a group: Create a spiritual fitness tip sheet, with ideas and reminders for how to achieve and maintain a healthy level of spiritual fitness.

At home: Take your spiritual temperature this week. Are you in need of spiritual medicine? Examine the health of your relationship with God, with others, and with yourself, and map out a plan maintaining or improving your spiritual health in all areas.

Prayer: *Dear God, thank you for reminding us of the importance of a healthy faith and healthy relationships with others. Help us rely on you to give us the nourishment we need to live healthy lives. Amen.*

Chapter 7
How Does Faith Help Us Rise Above Our Problems?

Snapshot Summary

This chapter shows us how faith can help us rise above despair, disillusionment, and defeat.

Reflection / Discussion Questions

1. Share a time when you were able to rise above a problem.
2. What are some of the obstacles that often prevent people from solving their problems?
3. What means of faith, such as prayer, can help people conquer the challenges of life?
4. What are some of the various sources of despair people often face?
5. Reflect on / discuss some keys to rising above despair. What has helped you?
6. What are some of the ways—in both words and actions—that we can help others who are suffering from despair?
7. What are some causes of disillusionment?
8. How is disillusionment both similar to and different from despair?
9. Define *defeat,* and give some examples of it.

10. Reflect on / discuss how faith in Christ can help us rise above defeat.

Activities
As a group: Locate biblical examples of people who relied upon their faith to rise above problems.

At home: Reflect upon the ways a strong faith can change your life. Pray, asking God for the courage and the conviction to follow the example of Christ.

Prayer: *Dear God, thank you for providing your power and your grace to enable us rise above our problems. Help us overcome the obstacles of despair, disillusionment, and defeat, so that we may change our lives and the lives of others. Amen.*

Chapter 8
Did Jesus Really Mean It When He Said, "Love One Another"?

Snapshot Summary
This chapter examines why common, ordinary people were drawn to Jesus through the power of his love, which is available to us today.

Reflection / Discussion Questions
1. In your own words, explain the meaning of "Christlike love."
2. Share a time when you experienced Christlike love.
3. According to the author, how did the Pharisees and Jesus differ on the concept of love?
4. What's the problem with limited, conditional love? What is it lacking?
5. What sorts of people were considered outcasts in the time of Jesus? Why were they attracted to Jesus and his message?
6. How did Jesus view people considered outcasts by others?
7. What types of words and actions make people feel welcomed, valued, and loved? Give some examples.

8. Reflect on / discuss the types of good news that Jesus brought to the people.
9. What risks are taken when we truly love one another? What are the benefits of taking such risks?
10. Give some examples of how Jesus practiced what he preached.

Activities
As a group: Use today's newspaper to locate acts of love.

At home: This week, strive to love *more.* In your thoughts, words, and actions, take opportunities to fulfill Christ's commandment to us, "Love one another as I have loved you."

Prayer: *Dear God, thank you for reminding us there are no outcasts in your kingdom, and that each one of us is in need of love. Help us open our hearts and minds to share the love of Jesus with others. Amen.*

Chapter 9
What in the World Are We Supposed to Do as Christians?

Snapshot Summary
This chapter looks at the alternatives for living in this world, including rejecting the world, resembling the world, and redeeming the world.

Reflection / Discussion Questions
1. How do you think "the world" views Christians? How are Christians often stereotyped?
2. According to the author, what are some reasons why the disciples of Jesus should be given an award for the "Greatest Comeback" in history?
3. What do we learn from this chapter about the early Christian monks and their approach to the world?
4. What aspect of worldly living would you be tempted to reject or try to escape? Explain your answer.
5. What are some possible benefits to a reject-the-world approach to life? What are some of the drawbacks?

6. In what ways are Christians today tempted to *resemble* the world, and for what reasons?
7. Why is resembling the world not a good choice for Christians?
8. Why is redeeming the world the best choice for Christians?
9. What actions are we as Christians called to take in redeeming the world? What challenges do we face in this mission?
10. What additional thoughts or ideas from this chapter would you like to explore?

Activities
As a group: Create "Help Wanted" ads designed to recruit Christians. Include the responsibilities and benefits of being a Christian and living a Christ-centered life.

At home: Look for those little opportunities in life to redeem the world and put your faith into action this week.

Prayer: *Dear God, thank you for providing everything we need to redeem the world. Help us be bold and creative as we seek to spread your Word. Amen.*

Chapter 10
When Is Losing Your Baggage a Good Thing?

Snapshot Summary
This chapter reminds us that we need to lose the "baggage" of closed-mindedness, arrogant pride, and ingratitude.

Reflection / Discussion Questions
1. Reread Hebrews 12:1-2. What does this scripture instruct us to do?
2. Name some common "baggage problems" that make life more difficult.
3. Everyone has a baggage problem. As you feel comfortable doing so, share a baggage problem that you struggle with.
4. Reflect on / discuss ways in which baggage problems harm us. How can our problems harm others?
5. Give some examples of closed-mindedness. Why is closed-mindedness harmful?

6. What do you think causes people to be closed-minded? What is the "cure" for it?
7. What is the difference between healthy pride and arrogant pride? Give examples of each. Can healthy pride turn into arrogant pride? Explain.
8. In what ways was Jesus a victim of closed-minded people?
9. What is ingratitude, and what causes it? How can we overcome ingratitude?
10. How can God help us get rid of unwanted baggage?

Activities
As a group: Using paper and pencils, let each member draw a piece of baggage and imagine that it represents one particular piece of unwanted "baggage" in his or her life. Pass around a wastebasket to let group members discard their baggage, ridding themselves of it in a symbolic way.

At home: Reflect both on yourself and on your life to identify issues or situations about which you are closed-minded. Strive to open your mind to new ideas and new people this week.

Prayer: *Dear God, thank you for opening our eyes and our minds to the unnecessary baggage we carry around with us in life. Help us lighten this load and become better at serving you and others. Amen.*

Chapter 11
How Do We Make Love Last?

Snapshot Summary
This chapter tells us that the best way to make love last is to love in a respectful, understanding, and Christlike way.

Reflection / Discussion Questions
1. Do you believe that lasting love is easy or difficult to achieve? Explain your answer.
2. Give some reasons why many marriages fail.
3. What does it mean to love each other in a respectful way?

4. What words and body language communicate love and respect?
5. Give an example of what it means to love in an understanding way.
6. Name an "empty sleeve" you have that requires understanding.
7. Who taught or modeled Christlike love to you while you were growing up?
8. What does it mean for love to *grow*?
9. Besides those mentioned in the chapter, what are some other ways to make love last within a relationship?
10. How does the idea of making love last apply when it comes to friendships?

Activities

As a group: Using art supplies, create symbols and messages that represent everlasting love. Share your symbols and messages with the group.

At home: Use your creativity this week to reach out to people who need love.

Prayer: *Dear God, thank you for love that lasts an eternity. Help us love others as you love us. Show us how to give love regardless of whether we receive love. Amen.*

Chapter 12
How Does the Christian Faith Affect Our Attitudes?

Snapshot Summary

This chapter encourages us to have an attitude adjustment to improve our helpfulness, gratefulness, and trust in God.

Reflection / Discussion Questions

1. Why is having a good attitude so crucial? How does it help us?
2. How does the message of Philippians 3:12-16 relate to attitude?
3. What is an "attitude adjustment," and why is it good to check our attitudes from time to time?

4. Are all attitudes a choice? How much say do we really have about the attitudes we possess and acquire?
5. Share a time when you chose the attitude of helpfulness.
6. Reflect on / discuss the importance of having an attitude of gratitude.
7. Why is it so easy to take life and its blessings for granted?
8. What are some creative ways to show gratitude and appreciation?
9. Tell about a time when you made a deliberate choice to trust God.
10. What are some of the reasons why we can always trust in God?

Activities
As a group: Reread Philippians 3:12-16 and personalize its message by writing it down in your own words. Share your paraphrased messages among the group.

At home: Take a reflective look at your own attitudes. Is it time for an attitude adjustment? What attitudes would you like to change?

Prayer: *Dear God, thank you for reminding us of the importance of a proper attitude. Show us how to display an attitude of helpfulness, gratitude, and trust in you each day we live. Amen.*

Chapter 13
How Is Love Best Expressed?

Snapshot Summary
This chapter focuses on how we express love through our words, our attitudes, and our actions.

Reflection / Discussion Questions
1. Why is love an important issue to discuss?
2. Share what you have learned about love over the course of your lifetime.
3. Why is it often difficult to find the right words or actions to express love?
4. Who taught you the most about love and loving? What did you learn from them?

5. Reflect on / discuss the encounter between the Greek woman and Jesus.
6. What are some of the different ways love can be expressed through attitude?
7. What are some words and phrases that express love?
8. Share a time when someone expressed love to you through an action.
9. Name some loving actions.
10. Why is love such a healing force?

Activities
As a group: Use art supplies to create valentines—regardless of the time of year—to give to someone as an expression of love.

At home: Use your Bible to locate biblical examples of selfless expressions of love.

Prayer: *Dear God, thank you for this reminder of the power of your love and how we can share your love with others. Help us risk unconditional love and be bold in proclaiming the love of Jesus. Amen.*

Chapter 14
What Is the Essential Spirit of the Christian?

Snapshot Summary
This chapter examines the meaning of *magnanimity* and reminds us to look for the best in others, to love others, and to be able to forgive and forget.

Reflection / Discussion Questions
1. In your own words, what is *magnanimity*? Share a time when you witnessed or experienced magnanimity.
2. What makes a person big in spirit?
3. Reflect on / discuss the connection between magnanimity and Christian love.
4. Is it easy or difficult to look for the best in people? Explain your reasoning.

5. Name some qualities and actions (words and deeds) of a magnanimous person.
6. Who are some well-known people today you believe have magnanimous qualities?
7. Why is it sometimes difficult to forgive and forget?
8. Name some keys to true forgiveness.
9. Do you think true magnanimity is in short supply in our world today, or is it simply that we need to open our eyes to see it? Explain.
10. How did Jesus demonstrate magnanimity during his ministry?

Activities
As a group: Brainstorm ways to increase the size of your spirit.

At home: Look for opportunities to be a magnanimous person this week.

Prayer: *Dear God, thank you for this lesson about ways we can act as magnanimous people. Help us let our light shine so that people may see Jesus in us. Amen.*

Chapter 15
How Does Faith Help Us Face the Storms of Life?

Snapshot Summary
This chapter shows how we all get caught in the storms of life, but in stormy times Christ comes to us in special ways. When we fix our eyes upon Jesus, we can do incredible things.

Reflection / Discussion Questions
1. Share a time when your faith in God helped you face a crisis.
2. What are some of the storms of life that most people face over the course of a lifetime?
3. Reread Matthew 14:22-33. What lessons about faith do we learn from this passage?
4. Reflect on / discuss positive ways to cope with frustration and helplessness during times of trouble.

5. How can the power of prayer help us during the storms of life?
6. Name some of the different ways God sustains us when we ask God for help.
7. Share a time when you felt the presence of God in the midst of a "storm."
8. How can Christians minister to others in times of trouble?
9. Why is it important to keep our eyes fixed on Christ?
10. How can you prepare in advance for the storms of life? What resources do Christians possess?

Activities

As a group: Search the Bible for verses that offer comfort during life's storms. Share your favorite verses with one another.

At home: Reflect upon stormy situations in your past and how God has been there with you.

Prayer: *Dear God, thank you for sheltering us in times of trouble. Help us face the storms of life knowing that you and your love will sustain us. Amen.*